WHEN COMMUNITY ENTERS THE EQUATION

WHEN COMMUNITY ENTERS THE EQUATION

ENHANCING SCIENCE, MATHEMATICS AND ENGINEERING EDUCATION THROUGH SERVICE-LEARNING

Kathryn Ritter-Smith and
John Saltmarsh, *editors*

CAMPUS COMPACT

www.compact.org

When Community Enters the Equation: Enhanching Science, Mathematics, and Engineering Education Through Service-Learning

Campus Compact is a national membership organization of nearly 600 college and university presidents committed to helping students develop the values and skills of citizenship through participation in public and community service. It is the only national higher education organization whose primary purpose is to support campus-based public and community service. Member campuses bond together as a coalition to actively engage presidents, faculty, staff, and students to promote a renewed vision for higher education — one that supports not only the civic development of students, but the campus as citizen as well.

Campus Compact is a separately incorporated subsidiary under the umbrella of Brown University.

This material is based upon work supported by the Corporation for National Service under Grant #95LHC0007. Any opinions, findings, conclusions, or recommendations expressed in this publication are those of the authors and do not necessarily reflect the views of the Corporation for National Service.

This publication was edited by John Saltmarsh and Kathryn Ritter-Smith. Layout and cover design by Lukas Hauser (www.getamac.com).

Additional copies are available for $10 from Campus Compact
P.O. Box 1975, Brown University, Providence, RI 02912
(401) 863-1119
(401) 863-3779 (fax)
campus@compact.org
www.compact.org

ISBN 0-9667371-1-3

PREFACE

As the only national higher education organization solely devoted to supporting campus-based public and community service, Campus Compact works with faculty, community-service directors, chairs, deans, provosts, and presidents to advance and deepen the practice of community service-learning at American colleges and universities. Our constituency is necessarily this broad-based because the pedagogy of service-learning, the practices of civic education, and the process of creating community partnerships for community-based learning requires not only a shift in teaching methodology, but institutional transformation. The Compact is dedicated not only to improving the quality of teaching and learning, but also to facilitating, even leading, the institutional change that is the necessary foundation for improved campus-community relationships.

Central to the teaching and learning mission of the academy is the quality and nature of the pedagogy that faculty use. What we know about faculty is that they work in a culture defined largely by their discipline. We also know that faculty adoption of service-learning has been most successful when the integration of community service with academic study addresses the particular curricular framework of a discipline or cluster of similar disciplines. Increasingly, faculty are also being asked not only to teach disciplinary content, but also to bring into their courses the additional strengths that students in any professional field are going to need in the world of work. In the sciences, mathematics, and engineering, while there is a professional ethic of service, there is an additional set of consulting skills increasingly emphasized as a part of professional development. Students in these disciplines will be required to have not only the "hard" skills of their discipline, but they will have to be proficient in the "soft" skills of communication, working in teams, multicultural understanding, and appreciating the ethical dimensions of their work. Service-learning offers a powerful pedagogy for teaching these students the skills that they will need to enter the new professional world ahead.

Campus Compact's efforts to advance and deepen the practice of service-learning led, in 1995, to the SEAMS (science, engineering, architecture, math, and computer science) project to work intensively within a cluster of similar disciplines to further the practice of service-learning. With a grant from the Corporation for National Service, Campus Compact subgranted to 175 individual faculty in the SEAMS disciplines for the purposes of curriculum development.

The faculty who received those grants have made a significant contribution to the disciplines in which they teach. *When Community Enters the Equation* includes essays from faculty who received grants under the SEAMS project. The richness and diversity of curricular innovation is worthy of a publication for use by faculty colleagues across the academy. They offer much needed insight into the rationale and actual practice of community service-learning, reflecting on its rewards and challenges, and providing compelling evidence of the power of this pedagogy.

Kathryn Ritter-Smith and John Saltmarsh, Editors

TABLE OF CONTENTS

INTRODUCTION 9
Rand Decker, University of Utah

MECHANICAL ENGINEERING 13
Why Service-Learning? And How to Integrate it into a Course in Engineering
Edmund Tsang, University of South Alabama

MATHEMATICS 29
Enhancing our Courses: New Dimensions Through Service-Learning
Joan Kleinman, Middlesex Community College

CHEMISTRY 43
Reflection in Science Courses: Is it Feasible?
Deborah Wiegand, University of Washington

CIVIL ENGINEERING 53
Professional Activism: Building from Service-Learning, Reconnecting Community, Campus and Alumni Through Acts of Service
Rand Decker, University of Utah

BIOLOGY AND HEALTH EDUCATION 61
Forging Effective Service-Learning Partnerships via the Cascade Model
Amal Abu-Shakra and Tun Kyaw Nyein
North Carolina Central University

INTRODUCTION

Rand Decker, University of Utah

Service-learning may be defined succinctly as integrating students' community service experience with academic study so that learning is enhanced and a recognized community need is met. The ideal is simple, and hence, compelling — improve the quality of the teaching/learning environment while fostering and enhancing students' sense of civic responsibility and agency. Within this context, service-learning has become a powerful pedagogy. There are now nearly 600 institutions offering over 11,800 separate service-learning courses in all academic and professional disciplines. Good ideas in higher education may find implementation throughout a college; great ideas in higher education find implementation across the entire university.

Introducing service-learning into the Science, Engineering, Architecture, Mathematics, and Computer Science (SEAMS) disciplines has required a little extra nurturing. To that end, The Corporation for National Service awarded a three-year grant to Campus Compact to initiate "SEAMS: Engaging Faculty in Solutions for Sustainable Communities" to enhance the rate at which service-learning is implemented in these disciplines. This publication, *When Community Enters the Equation*, is a compilation of essays from SEAMS faculty who present their arguments for the enhanced teaching/learning value of service-learning, as well as their methodologies and sample syllabi for implementing service-learning in their courses.

By design, *When Community Enters the Equation* has many audiences. Foremost are SEAMS faculty who are seeking an impetus towards the integration of service-learning in their own courses. Faculty life is not dull, nor is it characterized by an abundance of spare time. So why would one undertake to implement a pedagogy that will (it's a promise!) require some additional commitments on the part of the instructor? The answer is anchored in one's career interval. New faculty may find that service-learning can enhance their teaching/learning environment sufficiently that it will cast their classroom performance into a favorable light during promotion and tenure considerations. Senior and late career faculty may be seeking to re-invigorate their teaching commitment and skills in a search for that "spark of social conscience" that may have brought them into the faculty ranks in the first place. Additionally, there are successful, tenured, mid-career faculty who may find that the implementation of service-learning presents an opportunity to take a leadership role in the introduction of a modern, novel, and highly regarded pedagogy into their department, college or university.

Service-learning is a faculty activity, but it cannot occur without the support and concurrence of the other audiences of this volume. Department chairs, deans, vice-presidents, presidents, and chancellors — if you seek pedagogy and methodology to begin re-connecting your campus with its community, this volume is for you, too. Similarly, this volume is for campus/community outreach centers, the "broker" between community need and the faculty.

Lastly, but of greatest importance, this volume is for the disenfranchised people and places that service-learning, implemented in the SEAMS disciplines, seeks to impact in a favorable way. As service-learning practitioners, we can learn ways in which our work as academics has practical application that can alleviate suffering in both its human and geographic manifestations. Conversely, those who we are in service with, and the communities that we enter into, are our teachers — they allow us to discover the intrinsic value of our skills through acts of service.

WHEN COMMUNITY ENTERS THE EQUATION

MECHANICAL ENGINEERING

WHY SERVICE-LEARNING?

AND HOW TO INTEGRATE IT INTO A COURSE IN ENGINEERING

Edmund Tsang, University of South Alabama

Most engineering professors value experiential education where students learn through the experience of applying the theoretical knowledge and skills they gained in the classroom. Engineering faculty members who support experiential learning realize that the more "real-world" the experience, the more the students learn the subject.

Experiential education takes many forms in the undergraduate engineering curriculum ranging from formal internship/Co-Op experience to undergraduate research experience, design contests, project-based courses, laboratory experience, and field trips. With such a cornucopia of pedagogies already available, why should engineering faculty members consider service-learning as they consider how to prepare engineering undergraduates for the 21st century?

There is presently a paradigm shift in engineering undergraduate education, with inclusion in the curriculum of what some have termed "softer skills." Citing historical trends such as the end of the Cold War, a new global economy, and the growth of information technology, the Engineering Deans Council and Business Round Table of the American Society for Engineering Education (ASEE) issued a 1994 report on "Engineering Education for a Changing World." The report asks engineering educators to "re-examine their curricula and programs to ensure they prepare students for the broadened world of engineering work." (Joint Report, 1994)

Engineering Criteria 2000 (1997), the accreditation criteria established by the Accreditation Board for Engineering and Technology (ABET), formalizes the incorporation of "softer skills" into the undergraduate curriculum by requiring that engineering programs demonstrate that their graduates have, among other capabilities, an ability to function on multidisciplinary teams, an understanding of professional and ethical responsibility, an ability to communicate effectively, the broad education necessary to understand the impact of engineering solutions in a global/societal context, and a knowledge of contemporary issues.

This paper suggests that service-learning presents a powerful pedagogy available for integration into engineering curriculum to prepare undergraduates to meet the challenges of the 21st century. It also discusses how to integrate service-learning into the engineering curriculum with some specific suggestions, and outlines some of the challenges, concerns, and areas of scholarship.

WHAT IS SERVICE-LEARNING?

Jacoby gives this definition: service-learning can be defined as "a form of experiential education in which students engage in activities that address human and community needs together with structured opportunities intentionally designed to promote student learning and development. Reflection and reciprocity are key concepts of service-learning." Reflection upon experience is essential since it promotes "learning about the larger social issues behind the needs to which their service is responding. This learning includes a deeper understanding of the historical, sociological, cultural, economic, and political contexts of the needs or issues being addressed" (Jacoby, 1996, p. 7).

Reciprocity refers to the quality of relationships necessary in community-based education: "The needs of the community, as determined by its members, define what the service tasks will be. Service-learning avoids placing students into community settings based solely on desired student learning outcomes and providing services that do not meet actual needs or perpetuate a state of need rather than seeking and addressing the causes of need. Through reciprocity, students develop a greater sense of belonging and responsibility as members of a larger community. Community members being served learn how to take responsibility for their own needs and become empowered to develop mechanisms and relationships to address them" (Jacoby, 1996, p. 7).

Some guiding principles can be useful as faculty consider adopting service-learning in their courses. Howard identifies 10 elements of best practice in service-learning (Howard, et. al, 1993). They are:

- Academic credit is for learning, not for service
- Do not compromise academic rigor

- Set learning goals for students
- Establish criteria for the selection of community service placements
- Provide educationally sound mechanisms to harvest the community learning
- Provide supports for students to learn how to harvest the community learning
- Minimize the distinction between student's community learning role and the classroom learning role
- Re-think the faculty instructional role
- Be prepared for uncertainty and variation in student learning outcomes
- Maximize the community responsibility orientation of the course.

Further, implementing service-learning projects into the engineering curriculum consists of the following steps (Tsang, et al., 1997):

- Identify community need that matches course learning objectives, or vice-versa
- Form partnerships
- Create and implement solutions
- Evaluate solution for continuous improvement
- Reflection.

WHY SERVICE-LEARNING?

Any definition of engineering would include "service to society" or "meeting societal needs" as a mission of the profession. In the 21st century, the challenges to engineers in using technology to meet societal needs and human aspirations are formidable. The more obvious needs in America include rebuilding a decaying urban infrastructure, creating sustainable development, improving K-12 education—particularly in the areas of mathematics, science and technology instruction, and fighting pollution that impacts more heavily on those in the lower socioeconomic class. On the global level, the more obvious needs include supplying food, clean water and air, as well as energy for an increasing world population and fighting pollution that transcends national boundaries.

In meeting the societal needs for the 21st century, the contributions of engineers should not be underestimated, and not just because of the special technical knowledge and skills they possess. C.P. Snow articulated it best in his famous essay, "The Two Cultures" (1956), about the moral authority of scientists in meeting human and societal needs — which by inference can be extended to engineers. Snow wrote that

> the greatest enrichment the scientific culture could give us is — though it does not originate like that — a moral one. Among scientists, deep-natured men know, as starkly as any men have known, that the individual human condition is tragic; for all its triumphs and joys, the essence of it is loneliness and in the end death. But what they will not admit is that because the individual condition is tragic, therefore the social condition must be tragic, too. Because a man must die, that is no excuse for his dying before his time and after a servile life. The impulse behind the scientists drive them to limit the area of tragedy, to take nothing as tragic that can conceivably lie within men's will...It is that kind of moral health of the scientists which, in the last few years, the rest of us have needed most; and of which...we have been most deprived.

Future engineers will need more than technical knowledge and skills to fulfill the moral authority and to meet the challenges of the 21st century. The solutions to many societal needs require engineers to interact and communicate with people of diverse social, cultural, and economic backgrounds. Engineering education must be broader than technical knowledge and skills. Solutions to future societal needs require that engineers appreciate the power relationship inherent in implementing technological solutions (for example, who pays and who gains), and have empathy for the people impacted negatively by technology. Hence, engineers for the 21st century must have, in the words of Engineering Criteria 2000, "an ability to communicate effectively" and "an ability to function on multidisciplinary teams."

It is in meeting the challenges of educating engineering undergraduates for the 21st century that service-learning distinguishes itself from other forms of experiential learning in engineering. Service-learning offers a way to engage engineering students in thoughtfully organized "activities that address human and community needs together with structured opportunities intentionally designed to promote student learning and development" (Jacoby, 1996, p. 5). Through structured reflection, students can gain "a deeper understanding of the historical, sociological, cultural, economic, and political contexts of the needs or issues being addressed" — and can have an opportunity to demonstrate "knowledge of contemporary issues." Service-learning gives engineering students an opportunity to practice engineering design by providing services that meet actual societal needs and in so doing, they will have an opportunity to demonstrate "an understanding of professional and ethical responsibility" as required by EC 2000 (1997).

Ernest L. Boyer wrote in the Preface to *Scholarship Reconsidered: Priorities of the Professoriate* (1990) that many university professors "are drawn to the profession precisely because of their love for teaching or for service — even for making the world a better place." For engineering faculty members who are interested in helping engineering undergraduates develop a sense of community and citizenship, service-learning is an effective pedagogy.

Finally, there can be social benefits if more engineering faculty members implement service-learning projects into their courses, because many solutions to societal problems require the special knowledge and skills of engineers. "At no time in our history has the need been greater for connecting the work of the academy to the social and environmental challenges beyond the campus," wrote Boyer (1990). Service-learning reaches beyond the campus, addressing the need to broaden the community base that engineering colleges should reach and creating partnerships between campus and community. "A key element in the success" of engineering education reform of these efforts "will be partnerships: partnerships not only with industry, but with K-12 schools, community colleges, the broader university community, government, and among engineering colleges" (ASEE Joint Report, 1994).

IMPLEMENTING SERVICE-LEARNING

The daily newspaper can be a useful source in identifying community needs and partners, especially if your institution does not have an office of community service that can assist you directly. Many colleges of engineering have existing partnership with local school systems, which always have needs in courses in math and science. Local and state rehabilitation services often have needs that can make them potential partners for service-learning courses in electrical and mechanical engineering. For civil and environmental engineering, local or state agencies could be potential partners to meet infrastructure and environmental needs.

Two examples of community-based engineering courses, along with a description of how the course incorporates a service-learning project, are described below:

Course 1 - Introduction to Mechanical Engineering
Mechanical Engineering Department, University of South Alabama. Instructor: Edmund Tsang

A Community Need: In April, 1994, the Sigma Xi Chapter of the University of South Alabama held a forum to discuss ways the faculty could contribute to math and science learning in Mobile's public schools. At the forum, a panel of teachers, principals, and administrators from the school system explained there was a lack of resources to support active learning of mathematics and science. The resource needs include hardware (equipment) and software (activities and instruction manuals) to support learning math and science through direct, hands-on experience, and professional development opportunities for math and science teachers. Another panel of university faculty, K-12 teachers and principals identified the middle-school years as crucial to a student's continuation of math and science learning because elementary school students are interested in learning math and science, but their interest drops off rapidly by the time they enter high school.

Learning Objectives: In Fall, 1993, the faculty of Mechanical Engineering (ME) Department carried out a self-study of the undergraduate curriculum as part of a continuous improvement process. At the time, ABET's criterion on design was moving away from primarily counting the number of design hours in the curriculum to "design-across-curriculum." As a result of the self-study, three new courses with design content were introduced into the first two years of the ME curriculum beginning Fall Quarter, 1995. One of the new courses is a first-year, 4-credit hour "Introduction to Mechanical Engineering" —ME 125. Formerly, ME 125 carried only one credit hour; the self-study identified this format as inadequate in meeting the goal of teaching engineering design in Year One of the curriculum.

The community education need for more resources to support active, hands-on learning of math and science matches ME 125's course objectives of providing first-year engineering students with a "real-world" environment to learn and practice engineering design. The learning objectives for first-year ME students are to demonstrate successfully the engineering design process; demonstrate teamwork; practice communication skills (written, oral, and computer) and become aware of community-civic-professional responsibilities of an engineer.

The service-learning projects consist of teams of engineering students partnering with math and science middle school teachers to design and produce course hardware and software that meet the classroom needs and specifications of the teacher clients. Since there are many excellent, every-day examples of engineering and technology described by middle school mathematics, the service-learning projects allow the first-year engineering students to focus on the process and creativity parts of the engineering design process, without getting too bogged down in mathematical analysis.

The College of Engineering already has a good working relationship with the Mobile school system and its Southeastern Consortium for Minorities in Engineering (SECME) program. In Year One of implementation (1995-96), the teacher partners for the service-learning projects were recruited with the help of the SECME teacher coordinator from those middle school teachers who belong to the school system's SECME program. In subsequent years, the pool for teacher partners was expanded to include all middle school math and science teachers.

Service-learning Project: ME 125 has many of the same features found in model "introduction to engineering" courses described in the ASEE's 1994 Annual Conference proceedings (Gerber, et al., 1994; Hart, et al., 1994; Herzog, 1994) with the distinction that service-learning provides the context for students to learn and practice engineering design.

An orientation is held at the beginning of the academic quarter for the middle school teachers, who are provided with a description of the goal of service-learning projects, the project timeline, and expectations of the instructor, both in the form of a one-page Q&A information sheet, as well as a short presentation and discussion led by the course instructor. Faculty expectations for the teacher partners include meeting with the engineering student design teams to provide information and feedback; implementing and evaluating the hardware and software designed and produced for them; and participating in a debriefing at the conclusion of the project. The teacher partners are also surveyed about what they expect of the engineering faculty member and the engineering students.

The orientation is followed by a workshop led by a faculty member from the College of Education who is an expert in instructional design. Topics covered in the workshop include writing learning objectives and developing lesson plans for math and science, and issues related to mathematics and science education for the 21st century. At the second half of the workshop, the teacher participants write learning objectives for the service-learning design projects, and they meet with the engineering instructor to discuss their hardware and software needs to support the learning objectives — this is to ensure that the needs meet course learning objectives.

Students learn the engineering design process via two case studies during the first three weeks of the quarter. They are then given the assignment in week four, and guided by the instructor to complete the service-learning design projects in the remaining six weeks of the quarter. Some of the service-learning design projects performed by students enrolled in ME 125 between Winter Quarter, 1996 to Winter Quarter, 1998 are:

(1) Pencil rocket launchers and a simple sextant to measure the height of the rocket's flight were designed and produced to support after-school SECME activities for 2 middle schools.

(2) A flush-toilet was designed and produced to meet the needs of two middle school teachers to demonstrate the engineering concepts of lever and gravity-feed, and mathematical concepts of volume, the units for volume measurement, and algebraic functions. Middle school students use the flush toilet to collect, graph, and analyze data, and to develop mathematical models.

(3) Tools and activities to investigate the math and engineering behind the game of bowling were designed and produced. Middle-school students collect and graph data, apply the "ratio" concept, and practice spatial visualization.

(4) Tools and activities to investigate surface-area-to-volume ratio and its manifestation in the natural world were designed and produced. Through the activities, middle-school students practice the lab skills of measuring and collecting data, descriptive writing, and applying the concept of the "surface-area-to-volume" ratio.

(5) Activities based on building the Pyramid of Giza were designed and produced. Middle-school students practice skills in measuring and collecting data, applying the concept of ratio to solve problems, and practicing the skills of constructing a mathematical model.

(6) Based on the theme "fluids in motion," a windmill and an anemometer were designed and produced so middle-school students can collect data to investigate wind speed and wind energy.

(7) A solar cooker, a model greenhouse, and a support for a solar panel were designed and produced to equip an outdoor classroom at a middle school.

(8) Equipment and activities were designed and assembled to support an after-school science club where middle school students collect data to observe and verify Newton's principles on force, motion, and energy.

Course 2 - Technology and Society
Electrical and Computer Engineering Department, The George Washington University. Instructor: C. Dianne Martin.

A Community Need: Most community service organizations work with very limited or primitive computer resources that are donated to them. Some of them serve clients whose privacy might be compromised by the way the computer systems handle data and information. Most service organizations are under-staffed and their members overworked, so they can benefit from the recommendations and technical support provided by the students.

The community partners were identified with the assistance of the Community Service Office at The George Washington University, and included agencies that provide after-school day care, services to the homeless, senior citizen centers, an AIDS clinic, several public schools, and public health clinics. Each student team is also provided with an on-campus AmeriCorp student liaison to the off-campus community service organizations.

Learning Objective: An important idea that emerged from the 1991 ACM/IEEE-CS Joint Curriculum Task Force Report (ACM/IEEE, 1991) concerns educating undergraduates in computer science and computer engineering programs in which the social context and impact of new technologies need to be taken into account in their design, partly because of the ethical implications of their use, and partly because understanding the consequences of use helps to inform and improve design. An effective strategy to help students understand the interrelationship between the technical, social, and ethical dimensions is to have students conduct a Social Impact Analysis (SIA) in a real world setting.

In a "Technology and Society" course offered by the Electrical Engineering and Computer Science Department at The George Washington University, students work in teams to carry out SIA studies on how community service organizations use a computer system to serve their clients. This is a required course for second and third-year computer science, electrical engineering and computer engineering students. By carrying out the service-learning projects— the SIA studies— students will: (1) determine how the computer works in the community service organization, the actual vs. idealized practice; (2) develop a strategy to enable community service organizations and their clients to think about the social and ethical aspects of computer systems; and (3) provide the clients of students with a document that will be useful in future modifications of the computer system, and recommendations to help them improve the use of their computer systems to be more reliable, secure, and efficient.

Service-learning Project: The service-learning projects of Technology and Society class at The George Washington University consist of students collecting and analyzing empirical data of who is using the computer in a community service organization; how the computer system is being used to provide services; what impact does the computer have in the organization; is it viewed as a positive or negative asset in the organization; is the delivery of service being helped by the computer; and are there ways that it could be used more effectively?

Students perform structured interviews, surveys, observations, and content analysis of historical documents of the community service organizations and they complete the service-learning project by submitting a report and making oral presentation with their findings and recommendations to their client organizations.

EVALUATION

As part of the service-learning projects, students submit written reports and make team oral presentations to the instructor and clients. The written report and oral presentation can be used to assess student performance in meeting course learning objectives. One suggestion is to ask a colleague in the department to evaluate student oral presentations and have the colleague evaluate the written reports. Since the time commitment to evaluate oral presentations is relatively small (two or three hours at the most), it would not be difficult to find a colleague to assist in assessing student learning. This action serves two purposes: (1) The assessment results of the two engineering faculty members can be correlated to give a more accurate indicator of student learning — a strong correlation between the grade assigned by the instructor on the written report and the grade assigned by another engineering faculty on oral presentation provides more confidence in the assessment results; and (2) this is a good way to promote service-learning with your colleagues.

When asking a colleague to evaluate the oral presentations, it is important that she/he is involved in establishing the assessment matrix and that the assessment parameters be communicated ahead of time to the students. For example, oral presentations in ME 125, "Introduction to Mechanical Engineering" at the University of South Alabama are evaluated using the following matrix: (a) Overall Design - 30%; (b) Clarity of Presentation - 30%; (c) Use of Visual aid - 20%; (d) Team effort - 10%; and (e) Answering Questions - 10%. Students are also informed that each team has a maximum of 15 minutes to make the oral presentation, and should follow the format:

(a) Introduction — provide background information on how the project came about and how the team went about arriving at the solution;

(b) Describe the solution — provide details on the design solution;

(c) Evaluation — describe how well the solution meets the needs and specifications of clients;

(d) Recommendation — suggest ways to improve the design and/or its implementation.

In the quantitative assessment of student attitudes. I find that the method of pre- and post-surveys using Likert scales is not very useful as compared to open-ended questions in assessing the impact of the service-learning projects on the attitudes of those first-year students enrolled in ME 125. This is probably because the sample size is small (a total of 83 students) and also because I believe students tend to rate themselves "high" in the pre-survey, thus biasing the results of pre- and post-survey changes. For example, the reported changes concerning student attitude about teamwork as a result of the service-learning project as measured by pre- and post-surveys for the students in ME 125 is mixed and statistically insignificant. However, when asked to list three skills obtained from the service-learning design project, teamwork was mentioned approximately twice as often as any of 11 other skills. Teamwork skills cited by the students include "cooperative learning," "the ability to communicate with team members," "recognition of roles within the group," "working with others," "sharing ideas and working in a group," "designing a project to suit others," and "importance of total group involvement."

Similarly, the changes in student attitudes toward community service as measured by pre- and post-survey are also mixed. However, in the open-ended responses of post-survey, students listed benefiting society as a definition of engineering, along with problem solving and design. Benefiting society was either the most or second most important, according to student responses.

In open-ended questions, 14 out of 18 students in Winter Quarter, and 15 out of 18 in Spring Quarter, 1997, submitted written comments. Of the 14 comments in Winter Quarter, 1997 there were 12 positive comments about the course and two complaints about team assignment and about the amount of work involved. Of the 15 written comments in Spring Quarter, 1997, there were 12 positive comments about the course, two suggestions ("Change the project to high school students so we could delve deeper into more complex math concepts" and "make the course a 'writing' course."), and one negative comment about "the amount of writing required in the course." Some examples of positive written comments are: "I had a great time! The hardest work you will ever love;" "Excellent class that prepares ME students for the real world;" "I learned a lot from this class, like organization, communication, and how to get on your feet;" "Most enjoyable class at USA;" "Keep trying hard to do something productive for the community;" "I really was impressed with the complexity of this freshman level course. Students are introduced to the design process, required to write reports, and communication is emphasized. Without those items, engineering will not take place;" and "I enjoy this class and also am able to learn a lot of things."

REFLECTION

Reflection is that component of service-learning that distinguishes this pedagogy from other forms of experiential learning in engineering, but it also offers the greatest challenges to engineering professors. The goal of reflection is to increase social awareness and citizenship, and in engineering it is linked to developing students' awareness of societal impact of engineering and professional responsibility. Common formats for reflection in service-learning courses include essays, journals, and discussions.

Reflection for ME 125 is designed to address the goal of understanding the role of engineers in "meeting societal needs." In assigning the service-learning projects, students are given the reasons for the need for more resources to support hands-on learning in Mobile's public schools, such as minimum state and local funding support for public education, supply and demand for math and science teachers in Alabama and in Mobile County, and theories on teaching math and science. The course materials for the reflection writing exercises are taken from a section of the textbook by Raymond B. Landis, *Studying Engineering: A Road Map to a Rewarding Career* (1995). In that book the author identifies "giving something back" to society as part of development of engineering students. Students write short paragraphs concerning whether their service-learning design projects meet Landis' definition of "giving something back," and how the service-learning projects might help or hinder the students' personal development. Students were also asked to write a paragraph on what to communicate to middle school students — the eventual end-users of their design efforts — concerning the type of advice they would have like to have had heard from a college student, assuming they were the middle school students.

CHALLENGES, CONCERNS, AND AREAS FOR SCHOLARSHIP

Be aware that scheduling will always be a challenge with service-learning because your students and the community partners often have conflicting schedules. It is important to remind the students at the beginning of the service-learning project of the importance of scheduling, and ask them to be creative and be persistent in contacting their community partners, and making and keeping appointments.

Be aware that there are students who do not believe in community service and that some might even challenge you. One of my students was persistent in his objections. At first, he based his challenge on his objection to experiential learning for middle school students. He even stated that middle school students are not developmentally ready for such a pedagogy. I explained to him that he and his team could design a solution to meet their teacher/clients' needs using pedagogies that are compatible with his personal beliefs. This did not end his challenge. Next, the filed a complaint to the department chair by stating the design project was not related to Mechanical Engineering — he presented the class notes prepared by a guest lecturer (an expert on curriculum design for science education) on learning styles and instructional design as evidence. The matter was resolved when I asked for his suggestion to resolve his complaint about the design project in a meeting with the department chair; he suggested that the class should complete the service-learning design projects. I learned later that this student is a self-proclaimed disciple of Ayn Rand — he wrote a term paper arguing that being selfish is the most ethical thing a person can do, attributing three references to the writing of Ayn Rand. The disciples of Ayn Rand (i.e., The Ayn Rand Institute in California) are now formally challenging the requirement of community service or service-learning in higher education (The Ayn Rand Institute, 1997).

There are concerns about the idea of engineering students providing "professional services" as part of the service-learning projects. These concerns include: How "professional" a service is the service-learning project? Are students capable to render "professional services"? Would service-learning displace services of professional engineers? What about liability?

Service-learning projects cannot replace professional engineering services, which can only be provided by registered engineers. For community organizations and local and state agencies, which often do not have the resources nor the technical expertise, the service-learning projects do provide them with valuable information that can help them understand better the community needs or problems, and they can better decide if they need to seek professional services. The efforts of the students in completing the service-learning projects can be leveraged by the community organizations or the local and state agencies, such is the case with Decker Lake Wetlands Preserve Foundation in Salt Lake County, Utah, which is the community partner for service-learning in a "Hydrology" course to leverage outside funding to pay for professional engineering services.

For those projects where there is a slight chance of incurring liability, such as those service-learning projects connected with rehabilitation, physical infrastructure, or the environment, the instructor should consult the college of engineering policy regarding industry-sponsored projects, particularly senior capstone design projects. There may already be guidelines, at the college or at the university level that address the liability issues that might arise from the service-learning projects. There are few chances of incurring liability in service-learning projects connected to K-12 outreach, and those can be addressed by prudence and care of the course instructor.

Designing curriculum and course materials for reflection is a challenge but also an area of scholarship. It seems that a solution lies in the collaboration between engineering faculty members and their colleagues in the social sciences and humanities to either identify existing course sequences or develop new, interdisciplinary courses that support student learning about the larger social issues behind the needs which require their engineering expertise. This learning includes a deeper understanding of the historical, sociological, cultural, economic, and political contexts of the needs and the interaction between technology and society. Thus, the course materials will also address a curricular need outlined in Engineering Criteria 2000, of providing "the broad education necessary to understand the impacts of engineering solutions in a societal context" (ABET, 1997).

CONCLUSION

Service-learning offers engineering professors a pedagogy that can help their students develop a sense of societal awareness and citizenship to meet the societal challenges of meeting needs in the 21st Century. It is also a pedagogy that address a number of the student learning outcomes described in Criterion 3 of Engineering Criteria 2000. While service-learning requires extra work on the part of the instructor, the rewards of seeing your students learn and develop civic awareness and a sense of citizenship while meeting real community needs are well worth the effort.

Edmund Tsang is Associate Professor of Mechanical Engineering at the University of South Alabama. He has written and presented extensively on service-learning in engineering and has been instrumental in promoting service-learning as a strategy for advancing engineering education for the 21st century. Address: Mechanical Engineering Department, University of South Alabama, Mobile, Alabama 36688. Email: etsang@jaguarl.usouthal.edu

REFERENCES

Accreditation Board for Engineering and Technology (1997). *Engineering Criteria 2000*, website http://www.abet.org.

ACM/IEEE-CS Joint Curriculum Task Force Report (1991). *Computing Curricula.* ACM Press: NY.

Boyer, E.L. (1990). *Scholarship Reconsidered: Priorities of the Professoriate*, The Carnegie Foundation for the Advancement of Teaching, Princeton University Press.

Gerbec, D.E., D.N. Skillman and S. Conrad (1994) "The Implementation of Design Projects in a Freshman 'Introduction to Engineering' Course," *Proceedings of the 1994 Annual Conference of ASEE*. Vol. II: 2325-2330.

Hart, D., B. Engerer and D. Goodman (1994). "A Coordinated Freshman Engineering Program," *Proceedings of the 1994 Annual Conference of ASEE*: Vol. II: 2314-2318.

Herzog, .H. (1994). "Stimulating Creative Problem Solving in Freshman Orientation: Thirteen Practical Suggestions for Implementing a Successful Course," *Proceedings of the 1994 Annual Conference of ASEE*. Vol. II: 2309-2313.

Howard, J. editor, *Praxis I: A Faculty Handbook on Community Service-Learning*, Ann Arbor: OCSL Press, 1993, p. 5-9.

Jacoby, B. ed. "Service-Learning in Today's Higher Education," *Service-Learning in Higher Education: Concepts and Practices*, Jossey-Bass, 1996, p. 3-25.

Joint Report of the Engineering Deans Council and the Business Round Table of the American Society for Engineering Education (ASEE). (1994) "Engineering Education for a Changing World," website http://www.asee.org.

Kozick, R.J. (1994). "Electrical Engineering Laboratory for First-Year and Non-Engineering Students." *Proceedings of the 1994 Annual Conference of ASEE:* Vol. I. 63-67.

Landis, R.B. (1995). *Studying Engineering: A Road Map to a Rewarding Career.* Discovery Press.

Snow, C.P. (1956) "The Two Cultures," in *The New Statesman*, LII, October 6, p. 413-414.

Tsang, E. C.D. Martin, and R. Decker. (1997) "Service-Learning as a Strategy for Engineering Education for the 21st Century," *Proceedings 1997 American Society for Engineering Education (ASEE) Annual Conference*, Milwaukee, June 1997, CD-ROM.

MATHEMATICS

ENHANCING OUR COURSES

NEW DIMENSIONS THROUGH SERVICE-LEARNING

Joan Kleinman, Middlesex Community College

At a recent seminar on service-learning, the Academic Dean of a large college in New York asked, "How can I crack the Engineering Department?" referring to his lack of success, thus far, in convincing engineering faculty to integrate service-learning into their courses. Immediately, another seminar participant commented, "Yes, I have the same question. In my case it's our Math Department that is the one holdout at our school!"

How can we answer our colleagues' questions? What compelling reasons can we offer to faculty in the SEAMS disciplines to adopt service-learning? At the same time, how can we overcome some of the challenges that may discourage its use? Faculty, pressed for time and torn by many demands, need evidence that service-learning is a solid academic pedagogy that will benefit their students. Faculty also need to know that service-learning fits squarely into current thinking in higher education in general and into guidelines from their professional disciplines in particular.

In higher education there is interest in forsaking teaching methods that see the student as a passive recipient of information delivered by the professor. In an effort to encourage students to become actively involved in their own learning, many faculty already use strategies such as cooperative learning, case studies, and problem-based learning that emphasize critical thinking rather than rote memorization. Barr and Tagg (1995) have defined a "paradigm shift from teaching to learning" that focuses attention on active learning. Service-learning is a pedagogy that can certainly accomplish the objective of active learning.

Additionally, professional organizations in the SEAMS disciplines are calling for teachers to develop curriculum that presents content through contextual, real-world projects. A report from the

American Association for the Advancement of Science (AAAS) recommends that students should see how "science, mathematics, and technology relate to one another and to the social system in general" (AAAS, 1989). This goal is echoed in the document "Crossroads in Mathematics" (1995) from the American Mathematical Association of Two-Year Colleges (AMATYC) which suggests that two-year college mathematics teachers adopt a pedagogy that will "provide learning activities that promote independent thinking and require sustained effort and time so that students will have the confidence to assess and use needed mathematics and other technical information independently." The same document claims that "faculty must increase the mathematical power of their students" in order "to enable them to function more effectively as citizens of a global community where the opportunities offered by science and technology must be considered in relation to human and environmental needs." AMATYC's guidelines for pedagogy, including increased use of open-ended problems, oral and written communication of solutions, and a variety of teaching strategies, are completely consistent with the characteristics of a classroom that incorporates service-learning.

It is ironic that faculty in the sciences and mathematics have not embraced service-learning as quickly as their colleagues in other disciplines. "Why is this course relevant?" is a cry often heard in mathematics classrooms, and the lack of a compelling answer leaves many students unmotivated to learn what seems to them unimportant formulas and algorithms. In addition, science and mathematics phobia prevents many students from being confident enough to even begin to learn in these courses. Service-learning provides an excellent way to counter these hurdles.

Students from Unity College in Maine tutoring at a local middle school expressed in their journals "excitement over how well they explained a math concept." Furthermore, there were indications that "tutoring helped Unity students to 'learn to learn' math; watching the difficulties of the younger students gave Unity students insight into their own math learning experience" (Patton, 1996). A student from the course *Math Connections* at Middlesex Community College in Massachusetts reported using new knowledge to make a difference in the lives of children at the Lowell Boys Club. Students in an *Introduction to Web Page Design* course became passionately involved in their work in a way not likely to have occurred were they designing a hypothetical site for the imaginary XYZ Widget Co. In community sites students have opportunities to apply the knowledge and skills they are learning in the classroom to solve real problems for real people and to know that their contributions can have a tangible impact on others. They have an opportunity to see that the mathematics or science they are learning is useful and meaningful and not simply a graduation requirement or preparation for a higher level course. Service-learning provides students with ways of demonstrating — and using — their knowledge. For community college students with poor academic records and low self-esteem, this success is particularly meaningful and transformational.

Service-learning also allows us to rethink assumptions we have made about the nature of knowing. Parker Palmer writes that "the dominant theory of knowing in the American academy is 'objectivism', which claims that we cannot know anything truly and well except by distancing the knower from the known. Slowly but surely, that epistemology is being overthrown by the view that knowing is a dance between the subjective and the objective in which we need both distance from and intimacy with the known" (Palmer, 1993). Consistent with Palmer's observation is research from the Institute for Research on Learning (Eckert, Goldman, Wenger, 1996) which stresses the social and communal nature of knowing. Service-learning offers faculty the opportunity to counter the often negative image of the lone scientist or reclusive mathematician.

Finally, service-learning provides the opportunity for SEAMS faculty to incorporate an entirely new dimension into their courses, that is, the teaching of civic responsibility. It is in this area that some of the most significant—and unpredictable—learning occurs. For example, a student in an introductory computer science class assisted the computer specialist at an elementary school. The student, herself a mother of a young child, observed some aspects of the teaching and discipline at the elementary school that she found problematic; in her final journal entry she concluded that the service experience made her aware that she should take a more active and involved role in her own child's school. Another student, also a mother, reported over a year after her service that she was volunteering at her child's school because of the positive experience she had doing service-learning in her computer class. Students involved in a soil and water conservation and composting project in a conservation biology class had the opportunity to observe the "interrelationships between governmental agencies and agents, college and public schools, college staff and administrators, and faculty and local community organizations" (Patton, 1996). In short, students participating in service-learning begin to observe the larger social systems that are integral to their worlds. Through probing reflection questions, they can be asked to start thinking about the strengths and weaknesses of these systems and about their own role—present and future—in affecting social policy.

MODELS OF COURSE DESIGN

There are several models that faculty may choose to implement service-learning. An example of the required "one shot experience" comes from Chandler Gilbert Community College where students in an environment course spend one day doing field work and then use their experiences to prepare exhibits and materials for boys and girls at a culminating "Earth Day" fair. At this fair, the students teach what they have learned in their service to younger children and their parents. At the other end of the continuum is a course centered around service-learning where the site work is semester-long and required. Courses like these should be clearly indicated in registration materials so students know ahead of time that off-campus work is part of their commitment.

Another model — service ongoing throughout the semester but done as a option in a course — is often the most appealing to community college instructors who may be reluctant to require service-learning. Community college students lead amazingly busy and complex lives; most work, many are parents with attendant responsibilities and constraints on scheduling. A service-learning experience available in an after-school program will not be feasible for a mother whose children arrive home at 3 p.m. Indeed, in surveys asking why students do not choose service-learning when it is an option in a course, most cite lack of time as the primary reason. That said, faculty and service-learning coordinators need to look for community sites that offer flexible hours for students and that are close to, or even on, the campus so students do not need much extra time for travel.

When service-learning is optional, some students may hesitate to choose it because it is completely different from what they expect in a college course. It is only natural that it may seem "scary" to go to a strange place and meet new people. Other students may feel they are unqualified to serve because of lack of knowledge in the subject area and/or because of previous experience of the type required. For example, a student offered the job of assisting at an after-school program said she had no experience working with middle school aged children and therefore felt unqualified. To alleviate these kinds of fears, faculty may want to schedule a class visit to a service site so students can meet the community partner first hand. If time does not allow this, community partners can visit the classroom at the beginning of the semester. Students from previous semesters will make authentic statements about the value of service-learning to their peers. Also, assigning students to work in pairs, or even teams, alleviates anxiety and encourages creative collaboration. Clearly delineated objectives in the syllabus and comprehensive orientation sessions that prepare the students for the work they are to do and the types of issues they may encounter are extremely important to avoid frustration. For example, a student wrote in every one of her journal entries that she felt overwhelmed by her service because the initial description of the work was that of a teacher's aide, but at the site she was asked to work independently with small groups of students without constant and immediate supervision. Her expectations had been different from reality and she could not get over this disconnection.

CHALLENGES UNIQUE TO THE SEAMS DISCIPLINES

In addition to these general complexities encountered by faculty adopting service-learning, SEAMS faculty share some concerns unique to their disciplines. The following three vignettes exemplify a few of these issues.

Vignette 1 - Designing Reflection Activities

In her twenty years as a chemistry teacher, Mrs. Abbot has used traditional types of assignments such as problem sets and lab reports. Mrs. Abbot has just been to a workshop on service-learning and feels that it would be an interesting and valuable pedagogy. However, she is hesitant to incorporate service-learning in her own course because she is worried about using journals or other reflection activities that she has no experience designing or assessing.

Most math and science teachers are familiar with grading assignments that are content-based; they may never, like their colleagues who teach English, for example, have used reflection assignments that ask students to write about personal feelings and observations. Thus, like Mrs. Abbot, they may feel insecure in their ability to construct questions that will guide students to reflect thoughtfully and derive as much benefit as possible from their service experience.

For community college students, structured journals or paper assignments may work better than the unstructured journal which just asks students to record their experiences. There are numerous resources for guidance in designing journal questions. Hatcher and Bringle (1996) list many types of reflective journals including the highlighted journal which hones in on the student's ability to relate their service to course content, the critical incident journal which asks students to analyze a particularly significant event that occurred at the service site from several perspectives, including societal, interpersonal, and/or curricular. A three-part journal allows for an objective description of what happened, a section relating on-site experiences to course content, and reflection from a personal or professional point of view. Hatcher and Bringle also list other types of reflective activities including various kinds of papers, logs, discussions, case studies, portfolios, and class presentations. Reflection does not have to be written or verbal. Posters, photo essays, videotapes, or drawing symbols or pictures that are metaphors for a student's experience (perhaps in conjunction with a written explanation) allow students to express what they have learned in ways that may draw upon intelligences not normally evoked in the usual science or math college classroom (Gardner, 1991). Project-oriented service-learning activities are quite rewarding for both the student and the agency and produce an actual product that survives the student's service. For example, a nutrition class could create visual aides and/or written fact sheets for ongoing use at a senior center. Math students tutoring at an elementary school might build creative, hands-on materials to explain concepts to the youngsters.

It is, however, essential that reflection is tied to desired outcomes. The problem is that some of the outcomes of service-learning are difficult to measure in a quantifiable way. For example, how can we determine if a student has an increased sense of civic responsibility or an awareness of systemic problems in an organization? Asking a simple yes/no question is practically useless. Asking the student to rate her sense of civic responsibility on a Leikert scale may show some change, hopefully positive, if done before and after the service. But probing questions such as, "If you were the supervisor of your service site, what problem would you identify and how would you attempt to solve it?" provide the student an opportunity for much more critical, creative thinking and a chance to make explicit what he has observed throughout a semester. It may also lead to a sense of empowerment because it forces the student to begin to think about actively making a difference.

Vignette 2 - Making Time

There is a lot of material to cover in Statistics. Since it is a transferable course and also a service course for other departments, there is little room for flexibility in the amount of material or the topics to be covered. How can Professor Gilbert integrate service-learning into the course without sacrificing any time to cover requisite topics?

Professor Gilbert's service-learning students work in teams to do statistical analyses for a local non-profit organization. Fortunately, the bulk of the time involved in service-learning, the actual service, is done outside of classroom hours. Professor Gilbert can also ask his service-learning students to prepare their reflective activities outside of class, assigning these activities in exchange for ones that the rest of the class is doing. For example, in addition to their journals, service-learning students could give a short presentation of their work at the end of the semester in place of a final comprehensive project that others are doing. Alternatively, Professor Gilbert could substitute the service for one of the hour tests in the class. If the administrative structure of the college allows, Professor Gilbert might offer the service-learning as a 4th credit option or perhaps as an honors option in the standard course.

Vignette 3 - Doing No Harm

Professor Halley teaches Algebra II. He endorses the concept of service-learning, and the service-learning coordinator has suggested that his students tutor youngsters in the local middle school. But a major concern keeps running through Professor Halley's mind. His students, with their rather limited knowledge of mathematics, may make mistakes, teach incorrectly, and in some way do more "harm" than good.

In any subject area, in any placement, there is always the worry that students will "do harm." This is a risk of service-learning. However, it can be much alleviated by careful supervision by the faculty member and ongoing feedback from the service site. Students doing service may need to demonstrate in a notebook checked by the faculty member that they know how to correctly solve the kinds of problems they are being asked to tutor. The site mentor could periodically sit in on tutoring sessions not only to monitor quality, but also to help the college students with tutoring techniques. Finally, faculty who assign tutoring service to their students note that the students themselves are very conscientious about being well-prepared and sure of their own knowledge; after all, they do not want to be embarrassed in front of their clients! In a situation like this, there is a wonderful opportunity to integrate the work of the service students into the classroom. On a periodic basis, sample problems from the middle school could be solved by small teams in the classroom. Indeed, the entire class could be solicited for ideas about how to explain the material to the tutees. Service students then could report back their successes and challenges.

REDESIGNING CURRICULUM

When I was first introduced to the concept of service-learning, I decided to try it because I saw it as an opportunity to enhance my *Introduction to Computer Science* course by offering students new dimensions of experience and learning. Before service-learning, the objectives in my syllabus were completely related to content — knowledge of another programming construct or how to use one more debugging technique. Now my syllabus includes the equally important outcome of becoming knowledgeable about some issue involving the use of computer technology in society (for non-service students) or in the educational system (for service-learning students). For the latter, I've listed potential benefits that go far beyond the usual competencies of "just" knowing how to program, benefits such as increased confidence and comfort with technology, improved ability to explain concepts and verbalize ideas, acting as a role model for young people, particularly women students for young girls, gaining an appreciation for problems schools encounter in providing adequate academic support for students, and the opportunity to see if working with young people in an educational environment is professionally appealing.

I once heard it said that education is what remains after we've forgotten everything we learned in school. In truth, we do remember precious little of what we supposedly have learned—five years after graduation, how many of our algebra students will be able to recite the quadratic formula, how many of our biology students will label all the parts of a cell? My belief is, however, that five years after a service-learning experience, a student is more likely to retain content that he or she internalized well enough to teach to another or to apply experientially in a real project for the community. My belief is that the student will certainly remember that he or she "made a difference," and will know that his actions can impact on the community in which he lives. As Parker Palmer notes, service-learning "is an empowering tool that can help bring young people from the margins into the center, giving students both a social purpose and a sense of personal worth in the process of learning itself." While no one pedagogy is appropriate for every course nor for every teacher, service-learning is a pedagogy at least worthy of our serious consideration, whether we teach engineering or English, biology or business, physics or psychology. "When students move outside of the classroom walls to a community site," writes Palmer,

> they leave the relatively structured predictability of the classroom; experiences at community sites may be somewhat unpredictable and thus may enhance students' ability to be

> creative and flexible, to call upon classroom knowledge and personal skills to solve unique problems. At a service site, students are likely to encounter a diverse population which may be different from those in their classrooms with respect to age, ethnicity, social class. In a community setting students are responsible not only to the faculty member but to their community mentors and clients, thus fostering students' sense of personal as well as civic responsibility. (Palmer, 1993)

But it can do much more. The introduction of the community into the educational experience provides for new layers of learning.

Joan Kleinman is a Professor of Mathematics and Computer Science and Co-coordinator of Activating Learning in the Classroom (ALC), a faculty development initiative at Middlesex Community College (MCC), Bedford and Lowell, Massachusetts. During the 1996-98 academic years, she has been a lead faculty member for the SEAMS project as well as a regional leader in "The Faculty Role: From the Margin to the Mainstream", a Campus Compact National Center for Community Colleges program funded by the Corporation for National Service. Address: Middlesex Community College, Springs Road, Bedford, MA 01730. Email: kleinmanj@middlesex.cc.ma.us

REFERENCES

American Association for the Advancement of Science (1989). *Project 2061: Science for All Americans: Summary.* Washington, D.C. p. 5

American Mathematical Association of Two Year Colleges (1995). *Crossroads in Mathematics: Standards for Introductory College Mathematics Before Calculus.* Memphis. p. 43

Barr, R.B. & Tagg, J. (1995, November/December). From "Teaching to Learning - A New Paradigm for Undergraduate Education." *Change*, p. 12-25

Eckert, P. & Goldman, S. & Wenger, E. (1996). *The School as a Community of Engaged Learners.* Institute for Research on Learning: Menlo Park.

Gardner, Howard (1993). *Multiple Intelligences: The Theory in Practice.* New York.

Hatcher, J. & Bringle, R. (1996). *Reflection Activities for the College Classroom.* Indiana University-Purdue University Indianapolis: Indianapolis.

Patton, Monica (1996). *Snapshots of Service-Learning in the Disciplines.* Campus Compact: Providence. p. 4, 28-29

Palmer, P. (1993). "Is Service-Learning for Everyone?" from *Rethinking Tradition: Integrating Service with Academic Study in College Campuses*. Campus Compact: Providence. p. 17-18.

SYLLABUS

Ma 2101 Spring 1998
Introduction to Computer Science
Instructor: Joan Kleinman

Credit Hours:	3
Class Meetings:	Tues and Thurs, 9-10:15 a.m.
Location:	Bedford, Academic Resources 209

Text: *Programming with Microsoft Visual Basic* by Diane Zak, Course Technology, Inc., Cambridge, MA 1997.

Catalog Description: Introduction to programming using Visual Basic, an object-oriented/event-driven language. The course emphasizes planning and then creating interactive Windows applications. Projects will include the use of dialog boxes and of toolbox objects such as check, list, and text boxes, command buttons, option buttons, labels, frames, images, and scroll bars. The coding of procedures and functions will incorporate standard programming techniques such as declaring variables, implementing loops and decision constructs, and using arrays.

Prerequisite: Algebra I or equivalent.

Computer Facility: We will use Visual BASIC 4.0, which will be installed on the computers in the classroom.

Computers with the same software are available for homework in the Open Computer Lab, Academic Resources Building (Building 1), Room 212, on the Bedford campus. The hours for the lab will be posted at the beginning of the semester.

The textbook is packaged with a working model of Visual Basic 4.0, which you can install on a PC with Windows. The working model of Visual Basic is sufficient for most of the class exercises and homework projects although it lacks some of the functionality of the commercial version.

Materials Needed: You should have at least five 3 1/2 in. HID disks for use on a PC. A three ring loose-leaf binder is also required to keep printouts of your programs and handouts from class. Finally, you will need a folder with a diskette pocket to turn in homework assignments.

Course Goals: There are three general goals of this course. The first is to increase your ability to analyze a problem and to think through a solution in a clear, logical way. The second goal is to learn a new language, Visual Basic, through which you can use the computer as a tool to implement your problem-solving strategies. The third goal is to enhance your knowledge about computer applications through a research assignment and selected current readings or through participation in Middlesex's service-learning program.

Course Objectives: By the end of this course you should be able to:
1) Write an explanation of an object-oriented/event-driven programming environment.
2) Identify and state the function of the components of the Visual Basic programming environment and distinguish between design time and run time.
3) Identify and give an example of the use of each control in the toolbox.
4) Create toolbox controls and set their properties using the properties window.
5) Distinguish between properties, events, and methods of various controls.
6) Write BASIC code to control the events that occur when objects are activated including the use of decision constructs such as case statements and if-then-else statements.
7) Demonstrate an understanding of variable scope through proper declarations in procedures and functions.
8) Recognize faulty functioning and find both logical and syntax errors in a program. Use the HELP menu.
9) Choose appropriate test data to demonstrate program correctness.
10) Use the Windows operating system to save and retrieve files.
11) Apply the object-oriented/event-driven approach to problem-solving by identifying the tasks an application needs to perform, designing a suitable graphical user interface, listing the needed controls, and clearly stating the functionality of each control.
12) Discuss the use of an aspect of computer technology in education (as observed through a service-learning experience) or discuss at least one issue concerning the use of a computer technology in society (as a result of research on the Internet or current sources).

Your Goals: In the space below, please write down the goals and objectives you have for taking this course. What do you hope to accomplish? What needs do you want this course to fulfill?

Service-learning or Research Projects: You will have the opportunity in this course to do one of two special projects. These projects are outlined below, but are described completely in separate handouts.

Project Choice One: Do research on computer applications through two activities:
1) Pick a topic related to computers that you find particularly interesting. For example, you might choose to investigate an application of computers in your major or you might want to learn more about some of the issues concerning computer use in society, e.g. privacy or censorship issues. Research this topic by finding a minimum of five (5) sites on the world wide web with information about the topic. For each of these sites there will be a web site evaluation form to fill out as well as an opportunity to summarize the information at that site.
2) Over the course of the semester find three (3) substantive current articles about the use of computer technology. For each article, you will write a reaction paper of about two pages.

Project Choice Two: The second option you may choose is to participate in a service-learning experience. Service-learning allows you to use the skills and knowledge you are gaining in the classroom in the larger community; specifically, for this course, we will participate in either:
1) An after-school program sponsored by Girls, Inc. and Lowell Telecommunications Group or
2.) An after-school program sponsored by the Lowell Boys Club Association. These programs provide after school opportunities for students to learn computer skills through hands-on projects; at either agency you would serve as an aide for the teachers and have an opportunity to work directly with Lowell public school students. Middlesex's service-learning coordinator, Geralyn Vasile, will visit our class to describe the service-learning program and all service-learning volunteers will attend an orientation session early in the semester; Ms. Vasile will announce the specific date. Service-learning students will keep a journal, which will consist of reflections on their experiences.

As attachments to this syllabus, there are separate handouts that describe in detail the research option and the service-learning option. You should read both of these handouts carefully so that you can make a decision within the first two weeks of the semester.

Exams: There will be two hour-long tests and a final exam that is comprehensive in nature. Tests are announced at least one week in advance and the final is scheduled by the registrar during the final exam period. There are normally no makeups given for tests and you are expected to be present the day of the test. If you miss exactly one test, the final exam grade will be used as the grade for that test. Any other missed tests will be assigned a grade of zero. There is no makeup for the final exam.

Tests will consist of some paper and pencil short answer questions that will stress conceptual understanding of Visual Basic programming such as definitions, design issues, usage of BASIC code, and debugging. Some of each test will consist of short hands-on exercises on the computer, which will utilize material from the tutorials and homework exercises.

Grading:

Two Tests	30% (15% each)
Final Exam	15%
Homework exercises	30%
Tutorials	15%
Service-learning Project or Research Projects	10%

Ma 2101 Introduction to Computer Science Service-Learning option

Service-learning is an opportunity for you to extend your learning outside of the classroom while at the same time using your knowledge and skills to satisfy real, clearly specified needs of a community organization.

The service-learning option will require you to devote at least 20 hours during the semester at one of two community agencies that have expressed a need for help with computer-related activities. These agencies are Girls, Inc. and the Lowell Boys Club. They both sponsor after-school programs that strengthen and enrich the academic achievement of students specifically in the field of computer applications. You would be assisting the instructors in these programs. Representatives from both Girls, Inc. and the Boys Club will visit the class to explain their programs in more detail.

Service-learning will allow you to try an experience different from that usually offered in the classroom. You may have the chance to meet people of different ages and/or ethnicities; you will be able to apply your knowledge to real life problems and in turn expand your own abilities as you encounter new situations. Students who have participated in service-learning in the past have noted that community service has given them the opportunity to define their own sense of identity, enhance their critical thinking, develop their interpersonal skills, and develop a concern for social responsibility.

Some other potential benefits that might result from your involvement in service-learning are:
a) Reinforcement of your computer skills.
b) Increased confidence and comfort with technology.
c) Extensive practice in explaining concepts, answering questions, and verbalizing ideas. These are particularly important skills that are necessary in class when students work together and also in the computer field where most software development is done in teams. In fact, employers in virtually every area of the workplace stress a need for good communication skills.
d) Opportunity to share your enthusiasm for computers
e) Act as a role model for young people both as an example of someone interested in technical fields and/or as a student who has chosen to pursue higher education. For young girls, women students involved in service-learning may be particularly important role models.
f) Gain an appreciation for problems schools encounter, especially with respect to providing adequate academic support for students who may not be receiving enough support from their families and/or in the single teacher classroom.
g) Increase your interest in computer science and/or computer usage; you may be motivated to continue to study this discipline.

Service-learning Assignment
As you perform your service-learning assignment, you will write a journal in which you keep a detailed record of your experience.

Entry after each visit:
You will need to write an entry for each time you visit your service agency. You should:
a) Record the date and time of your work.
b) Describe, in detail, what you did and who you worked with. This is the place to write an objective account of the events that occurred.
c) Describe your feelings and perception about what happened. This is your subjective account of the day. Analyze and critically reflect upon your experience. What did you learn? How did you feel? What compliments and or criticisms did you receive? How did you react? What did you learn about yourself and the people that you work with?
d) Outline any specific activities you would like to do at your next visit. Are there any outcomes you would like to work on?

Final summary entry:
After the completion of your service, you should write a final summary entry in which you:
a) Summarize the work you performed.
b) Describe your feelings about your participation in the service-learning option.
c) Describe the benefits of your service to the agency. What impact do you think you had on those you worked with? What was your main contribution to the service site?
d) Describe how the experience contributed positively to your learning and to your personal growth. What benefits did service-learning give you? What new skills did you learn? Specify what you have learned that you probably would not have learned had you not chosen this option. What have you learned about yourself?
e) Reflect on any problems or negative experiences you had.
f) Reflect on whether this experience has made you think about possible careers in teaching and/or other jobs related to working with young people.

Submitting the journal:
Your journal should be submitted after every two entries and then again after the final summary entry. Journals should be preferably typed or at least written legibly.

Assessment of your service-learning experience:
Assessment will be a combination of:
a) evaluation by community agency supervisor and
b) assessment of the journal entries for completeness, thoughtfulness, and thoroughness and
c) assessment of the overall experience as described in the summary paper.

CHEMISTRY

REFLECTION IN SCIENCE COURSES

IS IT FEASIBLE?

Deborah Wiegand, University of Washington

Presenters at a symposium on service-learning during the American Chemical Society National Meeting in March, 1998, agreed that the reflection component of service-learning presents the greatest challenge to faculty who incorporate service-learning in their courses (*Chemical Engineering News* 1998). In each example presented, ranging from an introductory course for non-science majors to an advanced course for chemistry majors, faculty successfully located service partners with service activities linked to course content. However, the crucial step of reflection as a means to guide student learning was more troublesome. In 1995 the University of Washington Chemistry Department established a series of elective courses with science-related service as the central theme. These courses, called Science Service-Learning (SSL), demonstrate one successful model for incorporating reflection into a science course.

Reflection must relate to course objectives. In their study of reflection in service-learning, Eyler, Giles, and Schmiede (1996) found that students emphasize "...the importance of integrating what they were doing in their service with what they were studying." The type of reflection consists of describing actions and feelings about those actions and then connecting those feelings to community issues (Silcox, 1993; Jacoby, 1996). A focus on citizenship echoes the national discourse that sees service-learning as a means of enhancing civic responsibility among undergraduates (Smith 1994). However, in most courses, the objectives of highest priority do not focus on citizenship, but instead deal with disciplinary content and skills. Science faculty have successfully used service-learning to reinforce concepts (Miller, 1998; McGrady, 1998) and to build skills (Morocco, 1991; Eyring, 1998). Although some skills, such as problem-solving and critical thinking, comprise important attributes of informed citizens, the connection between application of these skills within the context of a discipline and their application to public issues is rarely explicit (Smith, 1994). The SSL courses clearly define both content learning and citizenship development as learning objectives:

1) Science content: provides students with content-driven learning outside the traditional academic setting and encourages the application of scientific knowledge in a way that connects students with the community.

2) Scientists as citizens: improves student understanding of scientists' role in the community and develops a sense of community stewardship and citizenship.

3) Community benefit: provides a needed service for the community.

Reflection exercises in the SSL courses address the three objectives above through site-specific discussions: class discussions on the link between science, education, ethics, politics and philosophy; essays on personal goals and perceptions; and a presentation summarizing the service-learning experience.

REFLECTION: SCIENCE CONTENT

SSL course reflection on science content serves to reinforce not only the concepts and skills presented in students's science courses, but also the process of scientific thought and work. Concepts and skills are developed primarily through site group discussions and then summarized in the final report and presentation given by each site group to the class. Undergraduates' understanding of the scientific process evolves as they witness the process at their sites. Students include thoughts on the scientific methods employed at their site in their final reports.

During the SSL course the nature of the science content learned depends on the activities at individual sites. For SSL students at environmental and biotechnology sites, the science content goes beyond what they learned in other science courses. Thus, reflection on scientific concepts and skills occurs naturally in the site discussions. In contrast, the service experience at K-12 sites where undergraduates are involved with instruction tends to deepen undergraduates' understanding of previously learned material rather than to introduce new concepts. Discussions of content learning occur at the K-12 site group meetings when the service involves the presentation or development of curriculum.

Science courses often start with a description of the scientific method, which undergraduates easily learn to outline, but the scientific process rarely relates to what they experience in the classroom, a litany of facts. In some laboratory courses undergraduates engage in the learning process (Kenney, 1986; Cooper, 1996) but more often the course appears as teacher-directed lessons with the successful students learning to follow the directions and those who are willing to experiment being penalized. What engages professional scientists—the discovery of the natural world—is lost for many students. SSL students witness the scientific process through either direct experience or involvement in inquiry-based K-12 instruction. SSL students at environmental sites are involved in the decision-making process of collecting and analyzing data. At the school sites, SSL students develop curricula that must engage K-12 children in the process of discovery. Thus, they deepen their understanding of how science is done by modeling the process in their lesson.

In their writings, SSL students report learning new concepts and relearning old ones. At the K-12 sites undergraduates often find they refine their understanding of basic concepts. One SSL student found that "...the difficulty of questions asked by second-graders seem more complex than the problems I'm assigned in my math and chemistry classes." Answering such questions requires undergraduates to translate their knowledge into explanations appropriate for 8-year-olds. From their experiences at environmental sites SSL students gain insight into the complexity of environmental systems. One undergraduate realized that the criteria for a healthy stream is not limited to only its appearance, and another reports, "I learned the cycle of events and cascading effects of an unhealthy stream."

SSL students also identify skills, both technical and non-technical, as benefits they gain from service-learning. For the environmental sites, strong emphasis is placed on acquiring the technical skills of use to the community, and SSL students do perceive that they achieve a level of competence in these skills. Undergraduates at the K-12 sites value the interpersonal and presentation skills they learn as a result of their service.

REFLECTION: SCIENTISTS AS CITIZENS

Common perceptions of scientists limit their role to the laboratory. The SSL class discussions attempt to expand this view of scientists to include societal influences on the scientific enterprise and scientists' role in society. Topics encompass science literacy, scientific ethics, science and politics, and science as a social construct. One of the essays and the final paper ask SSL students to elaborate on these topics.

Before the class discussion on scientific literacy, SSL students read newspaper articles: one that links scientific literacy to economic status (Peccei and Eiserling, 1996) and a second that argues for scientific literacy as a protection against decisions based on misleading scientific information (Glassman, 1997). The class discussion begins with a quiz consisting of sample questions from the National Science Foundation's science literacy test (Dietrich, 1996). The class compares their results with those of the general population and invariably the class has higher scores. The ensuing discussion revolves around the questions: why should all Americans learn science, what should all Americans know about science, and what can scientists do to support science education? Issues raised by students include examining whether science literacy is more important than other types of literacy, such as geographic literacy, and the difficulty of establishing criteria for literacy.

SSL students at environmental sites see the acquisition of knowledge of the environment as extremely important in developing these future citizens as stewards of their world. But undergraduates at K-12 sites go a step further in making the connection between this discussion and their experiences. They see the limitations of any type of literacy test based on a knowledge of facts, when the curriculum they are involved in emphasizes scientific process skills and critical thinking. Many students conclude that both basic content knowledge and the ability to critically analyze scientific information are needed to be scientifically literate.

The pre-class readings on ethics include sections from *Conduct in Science* (Benedict, 1995). In the classroom, SSL students go through a values-clarification exercise that requires them to rank the guilt of five people, all of whom share responsibility for the death of one of the five. In brief, a patient dies from a drug taken to cure a non-lethal, but disfiguring disease. The doctor who prescribes the medication cautions the patient on its experimental status. A drug company executive approves the drug for clinical testing, and a faculty researcher oversees the work of the graduate student who tested the drug. While the scenario is somewhat unreal, undergraduates take their rankings seriously. The discussion that follows highlights each student's reasoning and the underlying values that determine the assumptions they make. The disagreements that flow throughout the discussion illustrate the diversity of perspectives on what may appear to many to be a straightforward example. Students question the ethics of each player in the scenario, although the deceased patient is usually exonerated. Their ranking of culpability reflects their ethical views. One student's approach was to rank the five on the basis of litigation—who would be the best to sue. The class ends with a brief look at the process of making ethical decisions (Cambell et al, 1990). The SSL students involved in laboratory work have an easier time connecting this discussion to their service experience than those in elementary school classrooms. A student doing water-quality monitoring stated at the beginning of the class that he saw no connection between ethics and his analyses. After the exercise, another student in the class pointed out the ethical decisions a chemist must make in how results are reported—specifically in how the error in a measurement is reported. Other students jumped into the discussion citing examples of ethical dilemmas that confront scientists. The skeptical student, however, maintained his view that, because scientific facts are inflexible, ethics plays little part in a scientist's life.

Students begin examining the influence of politics on science through two newspaper articles. The first highlights the power of scientific evidence in the political arena, and the second reports on a study of how patrons influence scientific research (Oliphant, 1997; Stolberg, 1997). From this national perspective the class discussion moves to a local focus on one of the SSL environmental sites. A community group is working to persuade local governments to support building a new creekbed to move the creek from an underground culvert to a natural ravine. SSL students are asked to evaluate the proposal for both its scientific and economic impact on the community. Students who work at the site are more likely than others to support the community group's efforts to build the creekbed, even though the financial investment is significant. The discussion then moves back to a broader perspective in examining how scientific information and the experts who convey the information influence community decisions. This last part engages students at the K-12 sites as they see their role as crucial in educating future citizens to make informed decisions.

The last class discussion builds on the discussion of science and politics by examining whether scientific work is objective. Two articles (Begley, 1997; Burgess, 1995) present the debate currently taking place among physical and social scientists. In class, viewpoints vary from science as a search for absolute truth to all knowledge being relative. The discussion moves on to explore to what extent the scientific pursuit of knowledge should be encouraged. This abstract topic proves to be much more difficult for students to connect to their practical service experience than the discussions of literacy, ethics, and politics. Their strong support for scientific work appears to limit their ability to relate to the topic personally.

Most SSL students see value in the class discussions, but a few object to the "social science" nature of the topics and a couple do not believe discussions are a productive use of class time. However, after exposure to a diversity of views on controversial topics, students realize the importance of considering such issues in their future careers. One undergraduate found that the discussions "...helped shape a more rational and thought-out application of scientific concepts."

REFLECTION: COMMUNITY BENEFIT

One of the tenets of service-learning states that "those with needs...define those needs" (Honnet and Paulsen, 1989). In SSL, students establish a relationship with their site through a learning contract. In the contract the site coordinator identifies expected benefits from the undergraduate's participation. Site coordinators at K-12 sites expect SSL students will foster children's interest in science and serve as role models. In their writing assignments, undergraduates at K-12 sites do see themselves as role models, inspiring younger students to develop an appreciation for science. SSL students also believe that teachers and children benefit from the fact that, as a result of their efforts, more science experimentation takes place in the classroom.

Environmental site coordinators perceive that the SSL students provide education to the community about the local environment. In addition, SSL students are sometimes seen as agents to facilitate change and action in a community. As one site coordinator wrote, "This (SSL) project begins...solving the problem rather than merely addressing the symptoms." The undergraduates at environmental sites see their role as educators, making others aware of the environment, and as stewards, protecting nature. One student said that we have "the responsibility to take the methodology and critical skills we learn and use them to approach problem-solving in the community."

DISCUSSION

Through the reflection exercises in the Science Service-Learning courses, undergraduates demonstrate gains in both content knowledge and understanding of the role scientists play in society. The SSL courses are successful in raising the issues that will permeate students' future careers, but do not attempt to resolve these issues for the students. The process of wrestling with their responsibilities as scientists is modeled in the course with the hope that they will continue to examine these issues throughout their lives. In addition, the course promotes involvement in their communities as a way of responding to these issues.

CONCLUSION

Both goals, content and citizenship, are important. However, reflection exercises must correlate with the learning objectives identified for the course. The inclusion of citizenship issues as a course objective is appropriate for SSL as an elective course, but is difficult in a required science content course. Thus, a generic one-size-fits-all reflection exercise that relates students' feelings about their service experience to social issues is not tenable. For service-learning to succeed as an effective educational approach in science courses, reflection tools need to be developed that address the goals of enhancing undergraduates' understanding of science content and process.

Deborah Wiegand has taught in the Chemistry Department at the University of Washington, Seattle, WA since 1990. She has been the principle investigator on the Science Service-Learning project to promote experiential learning by involving undergraduate students in science-related community projects. Address: Chemistry Department, Box 351700, University of Washington, Seattle, WA 98195-1700, email: weigand@chem.washington.edu

REFERENCES

215th American Chemical Society National Meeting Technical Program. *Chemical Engineering News*, vol. 76, March 2, 1998, p. 56.

Begley, S. "The Science Wars." (1997) *Newsweek*, April 21, 1997, pp. 54-57.

Benedict, J., introduction, and Cohen, J., "Culture of Credit," in *Conduct in Science*, 1995. [Online] Available http://sci.aaas.org/aaas/conduct.

Boylan, P. and Ritter-Smith, K., eds. (1996) *Science and Society: Redefining the Relationship*. Providence, RI: Campus Compact.

Burgess, J. "A Dangerous Thing..." (1995) *New Scientist*, May 6, 1995, pp 54-55.

Campbell, C., Donnelly, S., Jennings, B., and Nolan, K. (1990) *New Choices, New Responsibilities: Ethical Issues in the Life Sciences*. New York: Briarcliff Manor.

Cooper, M. (1996) *Cooperative Chemistry Laboratory Manual*. New York: McGraw-Hill.

Dietrich, B. "How Do You Score?" (1996) *Seattle Times*, April 7.

Eyler, J., Giles Jr., D., and Schmiede, A. (1996) *A Practitioner's Guide to Reflection in Service-Learning: Student Voices and Reflection*. Nashville, TN: Vanderbilt University, p.18.

Eyring, T. (1998) Presentation at 215th American Chemical Society National Meeting, Dallas, Texas.

Glassman, J. (1997) "Commentary: How Gullible are We about the Danger of Dihydrogen Monoxide?" *Washington Post*, Oct. 21, (1997).

Honnet, E. and Poulsen, S.J. (1989) *Principles of Good Practice for Combining Service and Learning*. Racine, WI: Johnson Foundation.

Jacoby, B. and Associates (1996) *Service-Learning in Higher Education: Concepts and Practices*. San Francisco: Jossey-Bass.

Kerner, N. (1986) *Chemical Investigations*. Menlo Park, CA: Benjamin/Cummings.

McGrady, K. (1998) Presentation at 215th American Chemical Society National Meeting, Dallas, Texas.

Morocco, M. (1998) Presentation at 215th American Chemical Society National Meeting, Dallas, Texas.

Oliphant, T. (1997) "EPA's Browner an Eloquent Point-Woman in Fight for Clean Air." *Seattle Post-Intelligencer*, Feb. 20, 1997.

Peccei, R. and Eiserling, F. (1996) Literacy for the 21st Century. *Los Angeles Times*, Feb. 26, 1996.

Silcox, H. (1993) *A How to Guide to Reflection: Adding Cognitive Learning to Community Service Programs*. Holland, PA: Brighton Press.

Smith, M. (1994) "Community Service-Learning: Striking the Chord of Citizenship." *Michigan Journal of Community Service* 1, Vol 1, 37-43.

Stolberg, S. (1997) "Gifts to Science Researchers Have Strings, Study Finds." *The New York Times*, April 2, 1997.

SYLLABUS

CHM 197B: Science Service-Learning Autumn 1998

Dr. Deborah Wiegand, BAG 303c
Mark Kontulis, BAG 303e
http://weber.u.washington.edu/~ssl

Course Description:
CHM 197 is designed to introduce students to applied science through a service project. The course goal is to enhance the understanding of science and the scientific process through the use of experience and reflection. This class is designed to apply to all areas of science and should interest students who want to experience applied science and understand the fundamentals when working in a scientific area. Students will use their service as a vehicle to explore various areas of science and will reflect on their observations and experiences.

Format:
1 hour of lecture per week
15-20 hours of service per quarter

Grading:
This course is graded on a CR/NC basis based on participation, assignments and evaluations. To receive 1.0 credit in the course, students must attend the weekly lecture, do a minimum of 15 hours of service, complete and submit on due date any reading/writing assignments (reflection papers, learning contracts, pre/post-surveys, etc.), complete the final presentation and paper, and have a positive evaluation. You are also expected to come to the discussion classes prepared, having read the assignment and ready to share your observations.

Students who are enrolled for 2.0 credits are expected to complete extra requirements and are responsible for determining, in conjunction with the instructor, a suitable assignment. You may not have any unexcused absences from either class discussions or site visits. Assignments will be evaluated on content and clarity. Classroom and service observations will form the basis for evaluation.

Course Schedule:

Sept. 29	Introduction to course, site assignments
Oct. 6	Class discussion on service-learning and science literacy
Oct. 13	Meet in site groups – specific to site
Oct. 20	Class discussion on scientific ethics; essay 1 due
Oct. 27	Meet in site groups – specific to site
Nov. 3	Class discussion on science in the political arena
Nov. 10	Meet in site groups – specific to site
Nov. 17	Class discussion on science as a social construct; essay 2 due
Nov. 24	Meet in site groups – specific to site
Dec. 1	How to make an interesting/informative poster
Dec. 8	Class presentations/final paper due

CIVIL ENGINEERING

PROFESSIONAL ACTIVISM

BUILDING FROM SERVICE LEARNING: RECONNECTING COMMUNITY, CAMPUS, AND ALUMNI THROUGH ACTS OF SERVICE

Rand Decker, University of Utah

PROFESSIONAL: *of or engaged in a profession (an occupation requiring advanced academic training, as medicine, law, etc.)...*

ACTIVISM: *taking a direct action to achieve a political or social end...*

Imagine a situation where a dentist starts his or her work week by filling canceled appointments with children and adults in need of, but unable to pay for, dental care. These service recipients fill an otherwise unproductive time in the dentist's professional schedule and consume only a small fraction of the resources of his or her busy practice. A single phone call from the dentist's receptionist to a campus-based community action center provides the link between those in need and his or her practice. Staff at the community action center know the dentist and the dental assistants by their first names. In a matter of minutes our dentist has four new appointments scheduled for the week. The university's community center will contact the dental care recipients to make arrangements. During his or her academic training, service-learning had been a big part of the dentist's college experience. Our dentist discovered both the magnitude of the need, as well as the mechanisms for professionally serving his community.

Now imagine that this act of professional activism is replicated thousands of times a day in the offices and clinics of accountants, architects, attorneys, educators, engineers, health care professionals, and social workers. A common thread now links these varied occupations. A fraction of each professional's practice is set aside for acts of community service. They each maintain an on-going, post-graduation, "provider-recipient brokerage" relationship with a campus-based community action center. Each professional's introduction to civic need and responsibility was illuminated by service-learning experiences during academic training. In addition to the implicit, rejuvenating personal benefits of meeting a community need, the professional is also rewarded with tax credits, positive consideration from professional societies, and occupational and professional licensing boards. National calls to service and volunteerism no longer ask simply for your time. They ask for your most valuable time.

The arguments for institutionalized professional activism are so simple and compelling that they may have, to date, rendered the concept obscure. The powerful experiential teaching/learning environment of service-learning, coupled with that cadre of professionals who already set aside a portion of their practices for community service, further inspire the concept.

The shift away from public sector entitlements as the dominant mechanism for meeting our society's civic responsibilities has already begun. Filling the resulting void with an institutionalized, private sector response is one of the only alternatives. Professional activism provides a means by which private individuals with specialized training can provide services to those unable to access those services, meeting a real social need.

Students are predisposed toward the ideal of community service. Three-fourths of all entering college freshmen have acted in a service or volunteer capacity during high school. Yet we have failed to nurture, let alone institutionalize, this sense of civic responsibility as we move our young adults towards post-college careers. Only about one half of all graduating students participate in service and volunteer activities during college (Astin, 1996).

Service-learning addresses this failing and has become one of the most powerful tools available for integrating experiential teaching, professional training, and civic responsibility (and responsiveness) into higher education. Surveys of Campus Compact member schools alone indicate that there are now nearly 600 institutions offering more than 11,800 separate service-learning courses in all academic and professional disciplines.

Additionally, service-learning is being used to successfully address shortcomings in the science and engineering disciplines (Campus Compact, 1996): "Graduates are ill-prepared to solve real problems in a cooperative way" (National Science Foundation, 1996). Professional education must teach "students to work as part of teams, communicate well, and understand the economic, social, environmental, and international context of their professional activities" (American Society of

Engineering Education) and "to understand the impact of engineering solutions in a global and societal context, a knowledge of contemporary issues, and an understanding of professional and ethical responsibility" (Accreditation Board, 1997).

The service-learning experience, as well as the mechanism by which it is implemented on campuses, can be a preparation for institutionalized, post-academic, professional activism. Consider that in a service-learning environment, students who are training to become professionals "exercise" the learning objectives of the course against a recognized community need. That is, they are performing acts of professional activism as an element of their academic training. They are recognizing the need for and value of those acts of service that can be addressed with their learned skills. Early indications are that, in addition to the learning value, students enjoy a deep sense of personal benefit from their service-learning experience. We are training professional activists, but failing to provide the mechanisms to continue implementing professional activism in the post-graduate career workplace.

Herein lies the crucial role of the campus-based community action center in both service-learning and professional activism. Campuses with successful service-learning programs invariably have a community action center that can match a faculty member's course and learning objectives with a recognized community need. Not surprisingly, this same connection is critical for the successful implementation of professional activism. The community action center acts as an intermediary or "broker," if you will, between the community's needs and the service-learning faculty. This is a role that could easily be expanded to include "brokerage" of community need with post-graduate professional alumni who, by virtue of their personal and institutionalized advantages, have chosen to set aside a portion of their practices for professional activism.

In this scenario, where career professionals maintain an active dialogue with their campus's community action center, not only are the profound needs of the community being addressed, but also the near epidemic disconnection between universities, their communities, and their alumni (Astin, 1996; Boyer, 1994; Cisneros, 1995).

How do professionals ascertain community need in the very common event that they have relocated? Most professional societies maintain an arm or division whose role is to stay in touch with that profession's educational environment. If professionals relocate, they simply call the local chapter of their professional society, which in turn puts them in touch with a regional campus based community action center that can match their professional skills with a recognized, local community need.

Service-learning is here to stay. It is a sound, embodied pedagogy. However, it is imperative that we regularly remind ourselves that service-learning is a means to an end, and not an end in itself. One of the many desired outcomes of service-learning is a generation of learned professionals who set aside a portion of their practice to meet recognized community needs, that is, acts of professional activism. For clarity and discussion, these relationships between service-learning, community need, campus-based community action centers, professional societies, public sector agencies, and professional activism are depicted graphically. (Figure 1).

It must be pointed out that the implementation of professional activism is not, at present, assured. Can busy professionals be encouraged, by personal commitment, peer recognition and professional society inducements, and public sector privileges such as tax incentives, to set aside a portion of their practices to meet a recognized community need? An engineer would develop a "pilot" study to test this question by 1) finding a successful service-learning campus with a strong community action center and a cadre of post-graduate professionals who would be willing to act as the test population; 2) creating the linkage between the professionals and their alma mater's community center; and 3) oversee the results, evaluate the "costs" and benefits, and search for lessons learned. A scientist might ask the null hypothesis: "busy professionals will never set aside a portion of their practice" and then prove it wrong. A skilled social scientist could examine the process of professional activism in detail. The politician may examine the benefits of professional activism relative to the implementation of his or her strategic community vision, balanced with the need for re-election.

The purpose of this essay is to stimulate discussion and raise the issue of professional activism: What can be accomplished if professionals in their field are willing to bring the impact of service-learning to bear on recognized community needs through the institutionalized, lifelong commitment of trained professionals setting aside a portion of their practice to meet those needs?

Rand Decker has been on the faculty in the Department of Civil Engineering at the University of Utah since 1989. He is active in service-learning instruction and in the recruitment of new service-learning faculty with an eye toward professional activism. In the preparation of this essay he would like to recognize the collegial efforts of S. McIlroy, K. Ritter-Smith, and E. Tsang. Address: Department of Civil Engineering, University of Utah, E-mail: rdecker@babylon.civil.utah.edu

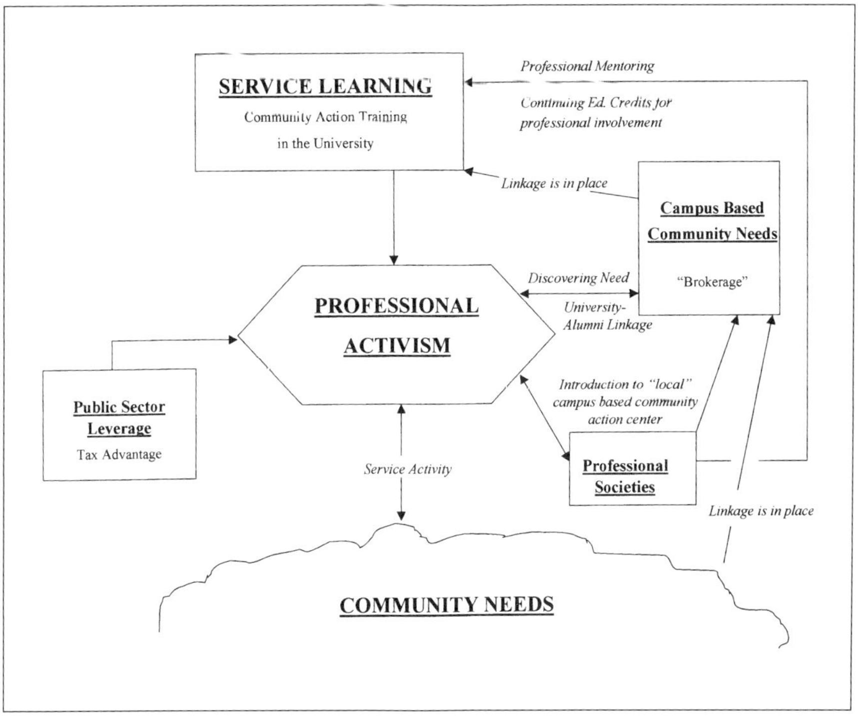
SERVICE LEARNING
Community Action Training
in the University
Professional Mentoring
Continuing Ed. Credits for
professional involvement
Linkage is in place
Campus Based
Community Needs
"Brokerage"
Discovering Need
University-
Alumni Linkage
PROFESSIONAL
ACTIVISM
Public Sector
Leverage
Tax Advantage
Introduction to "local"
campus based community
action center
Professional
Societies
Service Activity
Linkage is in place
COMMUNITY NEEDS

Figure 1

REFERENCES

Accreditation Board: Engineering and Technology (1997). *Engineering Criteria 2000: Criteria for Accrediting Programs in Engineering in the United States.*

American Society of Engineering Education (1994). *The Green Report: Engineering Education for a Changing World*, October.

Astin, A.W. (1996). "The Role of Service-Learning in Higher Education," *About Campus*, Vol. 1, #1.

Astin, A.W. (1995) "What Higher Education Can Do in the Cause of Citizenship." *Chronicle of Higher Education*, October.

Boyer, E.L. (1994). "Creating the New American College." *Chronicle of Higher Education*, March.

Boylan, P. and Ritter-Smith, K., editors (1996). *Science and Society: Redefining the Relationship*, Campus Compact, Providence, RI.

Cisneros, H.G. (1995). "The University and the Urban Challenge," U.S. Department of Housing and Urban Development, February.

National Science Foundation (1996). *Shaping the Future: New Expectations for Undergraduate Education in Science, Mathematics, Engineering, and Technology*, NSF 96-139.

SYLLABUS

Service-learning, Spring Quarter, 1998:
Civil and Environmental Engineering 452, Hydrology:
Hydrologic Analysis of Decker Lake

During spring quarter 1998, students in the Department of Civil and Environmental Engineering's hydrology class will be performing a portion of a broader hydrologic analysis of Decker Lake. Decker Lake is a 35-acre lake in West Valley City and is managed as a flood control/detention basin by West Valley City and Salt Lake County. The lake is bordered by I-215 to the west and Redwood Road to the east. It is surrounded to the north and south by the Decker Lake Business Park. The surrounding drainage sub-basins which flow into Decker Lake include industrial, residential, and undeveloped agricultural and former agricultural land. The Decker Lake outlet drains under Redwood Road to the Jordan River.

Over the years, Decker Lake has suffered the deleterious effect of urbanization, resulting in sediment filling in the lake and chemical/biological pollution. An on-going effort is under way to restore the lake and its surroundings by the Decker Lake Wetlands Preserve Foundation (DLWPF), West Valley City, Salt Lake County, and the local engineering consultancy of EMP, Inc. The DLWPF is a private, non-profit community service organization established in 1994 to promote preservation, as well as the recreational and education uses of Decker Lake and its surroundings. The

Foundation correctly recognizes that successful restoration of the lake will require integrated community and technical efforts.

Decker Lake is filled from a 10 (mi.) 2 urban watershed that is divided into five sub-basins. Several of these sub-basin are quite small and highly urbanized (~3 acre paved parking lots, for example). The outfalls from these sub-basins into Decker Lake are, for the most part, via un-engineered canals and culverts. There is one outlet from Decker Lake to the Jordan River through a culvert located on the east end of the lake.

One of the dominant questions of the DLWPF is the maximum lake level that could be realized under "worst case" inflow conditions. This question is motivated by their concern for flooding of lake side trails, and constructed facilities such as handicapped access, picnic shelters and interpretive, educational displays. The elements of a hydrologic analysis to answer this question include:

- What is the "worst case" cumulative inflow storm hydrograph from the five drainage sub-basins of Decker Lake?

- What is the Stage (depth) - Storage relationship for the lake itself?

- What is the Stage - Discharge relationship for the existing Decker Lake outlet, and what type of alternative, engineered outlet could be recommended so as to minimize the peak lake level?

In a previous service-learning Hydrology class, the land use characteristics of the individual sub-basins were considered, along with the hydro-meteorology of the central Salt Lake Valley, leading to the development of a "worst case" cumulative inflow storm hydrograph for Decker Lake.

In this year's service-learning Hydrology class (1998) you will bring your valuable professional skills to bear on an engineering problem of great importance to a non-profit foundation that is working to address a recognized community need.

Specifically, you will be responsible for determining the Stage - Storage relationship for the lake itself and perform the Puls (detention) routing of the "worst case" cumulative inflow storm hydrograph through the existing lake outlet, as well as through recommended, engineered outlet works to the Jordan River.

During the quarter, you will: 1) establish design teams; 2) develop "client-engineer" relationships with the Decker Lake Wetlands Preserve Foundation, Salt Lake County, and EWP engineering staff, 3) establish and document scopes-of-work for individual tasks; 4) perform the requisite analysis; 5) integrate the results of the analysis and make appropriate design recommendations; 6) present your results and recommendations to the engineering and non-engineering "clients" in an understandable and useful way; and 7) individually keep an engineering log to describe your work, the hours invested, and the impact you believe your efforts have had on the community, the practice of civil engineering, and the relationship between these two elements and your skills and commitments as a civil engineer.

Your efforts from this service-learning project will be evaluated and graded as the "design" homework project on the course syllabus (worth 1/2 of the total homework points available; ~50 pts). A citation will be placed on your transcripts showing that the course was taken as "service-learning."

In addition to exercising the learning objectives of the class in a realistic design environment, this service-learning project will provide a valuable experience in a typical "client- engineer" working environment.

Lastly, the service component of the project will give you the opportunity to consider how, after graduation, you might integrate or set aside a portion of your professional engineering practice for projects that meet a recognized community need, but are otherwise not compensated.

BIOLOGY/HEALTH EDUCATION

FORGING EFFECTIVE SERVICE-LEARNING PARTNERSHIPS VIA THE CASCADE MODEL

A MODEL FOR INTEGRATING SERVICE-LEARNING INTO SEAMS DISCIPLINES

Amal Abu-Shakra and Tun Kyaw Nyein,
North Carolina Central University

As the next millennium draws near, we find service-learning evolving rapidly and effectively in structure and application across the nation, and institutions of higher education are becoming more committed to institutionalizing service-learning and integrating it seamlessly into the curricula. Universities and their local community agencies are working together to encourage, assimilate, and promote partnerships through meaningful service activities. Further, the service-learning activities through these partnerships have never been more varied and diverse.

The steady growth of "learn and serve" activities emphasizes the realization that faculty and students are participants in creating a unique opportunity for learning. In adopting service-learning, faculty are doing much more than lecturing to a class or supervising student projects, they are making learning active and engaging in their local community. It is through their involvement that more creative partnerships are forged to involve university students and community partners in mutually beneficial service-learning experiences. Through service-learning, students are doing much more than learning theories and scientific methodologies. They are putting theories they learn in courses into practice, and using their education to assist community development.

This article focuses on the process of forging an effective service-learning partnership through a program design called the "Cascade Model." The model was originally designed by the authors for their SEAMS proposal in 1996, and was implemented successfully in spring 1997. The design of the Cascade Model of Service-Learning (CMSL) that links courses in environmental biology/health at North Carolina Central University (NCCU) with science classes at the neighboring Hillside High School (HHS) was guided by two central service-learning concepts:

- service-learning challenges the idea that universities can exist in isolation from the world around them (Mattson and Shea, 1997), and

- a service-learning program should strive to move the service relationship from charity to social justice (Watts and Nashman, 1997).

SERVICE-LEARNING CHALLENGES THE IDEA THAT UNIVERSITIES CAN EXIST IN ISOLATION FROM THE WORLD AROUND THEM

Environmental problems often impact communities that are the least able, politically and scientifically, to protect themselves. In such cases, universities can provide effective service by gathering the expertise on campus and making it available in a community-university partnership. Such a partnership becomes an essential tool in the struggle to find a solution to a pressing social problem (Benson and Harkavy, 1997). The expertise provided by universities that are committed to community service, such as NCCU, will continue to address environmental injustice in disadvantaged communities across the nation.

The CMSL was constructed as an environmental justice partnership between NCCU and the neighboring Durham Hillside High School (HHS). A large number of HHS students aspire to join NCCU upon graduation, and there are several academic programs at NCCU that are actively recruiting students from HHS and other schools, one of which is the Environmental Science Program. The CMSL project on Environmental Tobacco Smoke (ETS) and Lead provided a good platform for cooperation among the College of Arts and Sciences faculty at NCCU, the community service/service-learning program at NCCU, and the Durham public school system. Under the leadership of Chancellor Julius Chambers, NCCU is a leading member among the Historically Black Colleges and Universities (HBCUs) in commitment to excellence in providing the most meaningful service to its geographical community (Jones, 1998), and the service themes include environmental justice and environmental health.

Environmental researchers and medical experts who investigate the adverse effects of ETS have started focusing on the need to increase community awareness—especially among youth—of the fact that although tobacco smoking was not originally a major environmental health risk among American ethnic minority groups, the habit of smoking is on the increase among African American and Hispanic youth and among young mothers in the both groups. This condition is aggravated by fact that these youth are being targeted by tobacco company advertisements. Thus, a major task in the CMSL project is to initiate dialogue with the high school youth on tobacco smoking as an environmental health issue.

The other important health issue that the CMSL addresses is awareness of lingering problem of lead poisoning. It is a fact that the adverse health effects of exposure to lead range from detectable behavioral and mental disorders, especially in children (0 to 5 years), to acute toxicity and death. Lead poisoning is more associated with economically disadvantaged communities that are also predominantly African American and Hispanic. This is the socioeconomic profile in Northeast/Central Durham, and the Durham's Eagle Village, the neighborhood that surrounds NCCU.

The NCCU faculty facilitated the effort of the NCCU students to disseminate information on the two environmental pollutants (ETS and Lead) to the youth of the community at HHS. It was by design that the CMSL focused on students spearheading the service-learning community-university dialogue activities. Students, the servers/learners from NCCU, planned, mediated, and directed discussions that took place in classes at the high school. The students tackled many sensitive issues, such as the concern that cigarette company advertisements target minority teenagers and health care concerns ranging from inaccurate diagnosis to diminished access to medical treatment. This was followed by discussions of the impact of peer-pressure on programs that promote prevention of tobacco smoking or smoking cessation. Finally, students discussed the value of education in the process of seeking health and wellness, and the prevention of environment pollution.

The performance of all the students involved was impressive and reflected growing civic responsibility. More importantly, the faculty realized from observations in the class and from reflections during and after the dialogue sessions that the students thrived when fresh angles of discussion emerged. The dialogue on health and wellness reached the understanding that the picture gets clearer when more scientific findings come to light, and that on-going research is a necessary activity. Their discussion was on the mind of many of the CMSL participants when recent research findings from the Centers for Disease Control and Prevention confirmed that the health hazards caused by smoking are noticeably greater among African Americans than whites, and that more research is needed to clarify this medical question. The students had it right.

Lead poisoning is more concentrated among the children of residents of low income housing in urban settings. The youth at the high school showed excellent responsiveness to the service-learning goal of increasing awareness of lingering problem of lead poisoning to help reduce its harmful impact on the community, especially the children. The students gained awareness that most of the old houses in Durham are inhabited by families that can ill-afford to add the health burden from lead poisoning to all the other health risks faced by them and their children due to environmental pollution. With service-learning, the students learn not only about problems, but also engage in creating solutions. Therefore, activities that contributed to the solution quickly became part of the students repertoire in this service-learning project and included community outreach, surveys and questionnaires, and research.

A SERVICE-LEARNING PROGRAM SHOULD STRIVE TO MOVE THE SERVICE RELATIONSHIP FROM CHARITY TO SOCIAL JUSTICE

Striving for social justice fits well with the mission of NCCU. The university has been championing many causes, and among these is the immediate need to enhance health and wellness in communities that are most afflicted by environmental pollution and its harmful effects. It is evident that the Durham community is interested in partnering with NCCU around issues of environmental and social justice.

The Cascade model, as a tool to promote social justice, employs service-learning in a range of courses all with a common goal of disseminating student-gathered information on the health effects associated with exposure to ETS and lead. The students' approach to the course reflected growing enthusiasm and commitment to sensitive issues ranging from child health to environmental justice. The multilevel format of the CMSL learning that was implemented in spring 1997 started with the junior/senior level Biology (Bio 2700; Environmental Problems) course as the first of a sequence. The second and third courses were a freshman-level Health and Wellness (CFAS 1530) course and two science classes at HHS, respectively. Finally, the model extended to the Durham community schools and day care centers among others.

The Environmental Problems course is a Biology elective at NCCU and is a core course within the Environmental Science Degree program. It has a dynamic syllabus that includes a service-learning project. Through this project, students put their environmental science knowledge to use by tackling several need-based and community-oriented environmental issues. In 1996, the students worked on enhancing community awareness to Legionnaires Disease, and their effort won a national award (Boylan and Ritter-Smith, 1996).

For the Health and Wellness (CFAS 1530) students, the project offered an opportunity to experience truly interdisciplinary instruction and the benefit of service-learning training at an early stage in their university experience. The CFAS acronym stands for Critical Foundations in the Arts and Sciences, which is an innovative undergraduate program offered within the NCCU College of Arts and Sciences. The CFAS Health and Wellness component is offered in part within the Department of Health Education that has been a traditional provider of health-related services to the community in Durham and beyond. The service-learning partnership between NCCU and the high school was achieved by connecting both university courses with the environmental science classes and the International Baccalaureate science classes at Durham's HHS. The smooth transition between university and high school was pivotal for the success of the model.

For their service-learning project, students selected to work in five groups to perform many tasks all aimed at achieving environmental/social justice. These tasks included the following: working with the NCCU community and the larger community through interviews to get a feel of the problem as seen by the community; using the current scientific literature and statistical studies to generate the questionnaire; analyzing data collected from the questionnaires; conducting a thorough search of the literature, in scientific journals and on-line; and producing a sophisticated and helpful teaching tool in the form of a brochure titled "Indoor Air Safety: Lead and Environmental Tobacco Smoke." This user-friendly brochure was provided to many community agencies and schools to furnish necessary information on environmental pollution related to ETS and lead, including charts, Internet URL addresses and telephone numbers.

The NCCU students as well as HHS students emerged as individuals with training that (a) is relevant to the community and (b) offers a potential for future careers. The students demonstrated heightened awareness to community needs. More strikingly, the reflections of the students collected on video and audio tapes and in writing demonstrated a major impact of service-learning experiences on the emergence of a sense of responsibility associated with knowledge, as observed by Mattson and Shea (1997).

PARTNERSHIPS FORGED USING THE CASCADE MODEL

Universities can partner with local communities in supporting social justice through civic responsibility and environmental equity. The Cascade Model can be an effective way of connecting university curricula and community activities, and the model in its more extendable form (accordion-like) can go beyond high schools and into middle schools and elementary schools.

Currently, the model connects NCCU in a partnership with the Durham school system (HHS and five elementary schools), the Durham Child Care Council, Operation Breakthrough, and the health department. Students are actively involved a project that addresses environmental safety and educational issues. This initiative has led to a workshop on the "Art of Partnering: Best Practices and Lessons Learned." Participants shared their experiences on creating, managing, and maintaining partnerships. In addition, strong emphasis will be put on the evaluation of partnerships.

One of the major community-university partnerships highlighted at the Art of Partnering workshop was a partnership that involved NCCU directly with environmental and social justice: the "Partnership Effort for the Advancement of Children Health (PEACH). This PEACH project was funded by a the Environmental Justice Office of the US Environmental Protection Agency to reduce the exposure of children to the harmful effects of lead in Northeast Central Durham (NECD) homes.

In the PEACH partnership, NCCU faculty and students are not only working on the educational aspects and the scientific analyses and measurement of environmental pollution, but they are also learning the art of partnering with the NECD community through direct interaction with the community groups who are involved in the house-to-house education and the intervention activities.

Lastly, in response to future community needs and in an true effort to promote social justice in the next century, the CMSL is being tested as a partnership model for incorporating information technology in instruction and service. The technological revolution has been quickly embraced, and computer and Internet usage is rapidly spreading. Given these facts, and the understanding that NCCU is committed to serving and enhancing the cultural, social and economic well-being of the community through university/community partnerships, the advent of the "Age of Information" will be felt in the incorporation of information technology-based service-learning instruction in Biology and health courses.

Dr. Amal Abu-Shakra joined the faculty of the Department of Biology at North Carolina Central University in fall 1994. Dr. Abu-Shakra became involved in service at NCCU, serving as the Biology Department CS/service-learning liaison and as Co-Chair of the NCCU Faculty/Administrators service-learning Fellows Program (FASLF). Dr. Abu-Shakra has pursued (a) the adoption of service-learning as a tool for university-community partnering and a strong linker of interdisciplinary curricula, and (b) strengthening the efforts to institutionalize service-learning at NCCU.

Dr. Tun Kyaw Nyein joined the faculty of the Department of Health Education in 1993. Dr. Nyein is an active participant in the FASLF Program, and has been playing a pioneering role in promoting distance learning through the incorporation of information technology in the curriculum at NCCU.

The authors would like to acknowledge the leadership of Chancellor Julius Chambers in promoting service-learning at NCCU ; the guidance and advice of Dr. Beverly Washington-Jones, who has been a powerful force behind the sustained growth of service-learning at NCCU; and the cooperation of Mr. Kenneth Cutler, whose efforts contributed greatly to the success of the application of Cascade model.

Address: Biology Department, North Carolina Central University,Durham, NC 27707, E-mail: abushak@wpo.nccu.edu

REFERENCES:

Benson, L. and Harkavy, I , eds. (1997) "Universities, Colleges and their Neighboring Communities", in *Universities and Community Schools*, Vol. 5: 5-11.

Boylan, P. and Ritter-Smith, K., eds. (1996) *Science and Society: Redefining the Relationship*. Campus Compact, Providence, RI, 26-30.

Jones. B.W. (1998) "Rediscovering our Heritage: Community Service and the Historically Black University," in Zlotkowski, E., ed., *Successful Service-Learning Programs: New Models of Excellence in Higher Education*. Anker Publishing Co., Bolton MA, 109-122.

Mattson, K. and Shea, M. (1997) "The Selling of Service-Learning to the Modern University: How Much Will it Cost?" in *Expanding Boundaries: Building Civic Responsibility Within Higher Education*, The Corporation for National Service; Washington, DC. Vol. 2: 12-19.

Watts, T. and Nashman, H. (1997) "Taking the Next Step: Fostering University-Community Collaboration that Reach Beyond Service-Learning." in *Expanding Boundaries: Building Civic Responsibility within Higher Education*, The Corporation for National Service; Washington, DC. Vol. 2:26-28.

SYLLABUS

Environmental Problems, BIO 2700
North Carolina Central University
Department of Biology

Instructor: Dr. Amal Abu-Shakra
Office Location: Lee Biology Building Rm. 115
E-Mail: abushak@wpo.nccu.edu

"Advancing Teaching, Scholarship, and Service through Diversity, Partnerships, and Technology"

Course Description:
Junior/Senior Biology Elective for Biology Majors
Core Course for Environmental Science Majors

This course is designed to provide students with intensive instruction in the following: (1) causes, effects, and solutions of environmental problems, (2) modern techniques developed to detect and investigate environmental damage, and (3) emerging policies on environmental protection and community health, locally and globally. Students sit through course lectures, seminars, slide sessions, and invited lectures to learn about all five sections of the course which are: Air Quality, Water Quality, Occupational Hazards, Environmental Research, and Community Environmental Health.

Number of Credit Hours: 4 credits (Spring Semester)

Required Text: Environmental Science: A Global Concern, Cunningham and Saigo, 4th Edition, Wm.C. Brown Publishers.

Common Themes for the Course:
The following themes are common to all five sections of the course:

- service-learning; Community/University partnership;
- Technological advances;
- Environmental justice; Global Concerns
- Course Competencies and Objectives/Course

Outcomes:

To offer students a panoramic view of a world under environmental stress, and encourage them to think of global environmental problems.

To train students to analyze individual environmental problems using the scientific method from various angles: biological, chemical, physical, geographical, economical and political.

To empower students to be objective investigators in environmental science, while drawing on personal experiences and community interests and needs.

To identify problems and select projects that may affect their lives directly.

To encourage students to probe into the various aspects of modern environmental research, which for some may influence future career choices.

To ensure that students develop growing awareness about environmental health & justice, and translate that to community benefit through community service/service-learning activities.

To introduce students to many of the agencies, laboratories, and international organizations that play major parts in structuring environmental policies.

Topical Outline with Dates:

Week 1: INTRODUCTION

Presentation of a global picture of the environment using a simple schematic diagram. Explaining the basic principles that govern the environment and its dynamic balance. Introducing sources and samples of the literature: e.g.
journal articles.

Week 2 - Week 4 AIR QUALITY:

Pollutants in Air: Chemical and Biological Health Hazards
Topics in Air pollution: Environmental Tobacco Smoke (ETS), Automobile and Incinerator Emissions, toxic industrial gases. Air pollution Accidents, such as Chernobyl, Love Canal, Seveso, and Three Mile Island. Presentation and discussion of literature Emerging concerns in Air Quality: The hole in the ozone, The Greenhouse effect, Global warming.

Week 5 - Week 7 WATER QUALITY:

Pollutants in Water: Chemical & Biological health hazards.
Industrial pollutants: chemical classes, sources, detection, and impact on the environment. Making drinking water safe Global Problems: Water shortage, ocean dumping, point and non-point sources.

Week 8 - Week 10 OCCUPATIONAL HAZARDS:

Overview of occupational hazards.

Radiation in the work place: Safe handling and record keeping. Introduction to Chemical Carcinogenesis. Pesticides: a major environmental problem
Sick Building Syndrome: causes, health impacts, and solutions.

Week 11- Week 13 ENVIRONMENTAL RESEARCH:

Introduction to Environmental Research. Classic vs. current trends in research. Collection of environmental samples: General principles, definitions and schematic diagrams. Complex Environmental Mixtures: Extraction/purification techniques. Principles of High Performance [Pressure] Liquid Chromatography Environmental Toxicology: Salmonella mutation assay (Ames Test) and Transgenic systems. Introduction to molecular biology: Techniques in Environmental Toxicology Labs.

Week 14 COMMUNITY HEALTH:

Defining Community Health from an environmental angle
Adverse health effects related to air and water pollution Environmental Solutions: U.S. Environmental Protection Agency (EPA). Environmental Education & Environmental Justice

The service-learning component of Biology 2700:

Service-learning (service-learning) is an educational strategy by which students develop active participation in thoroughly organized public service activities. Meaningful service-learning meets community needs, helps foster civic responsibility, enhances the academic curriculum, and integrates structured time for the students and participants to reflect on the service-learning experiences. Themes of the Biology 2700 service-learning projects can span the five sections of the course. Since Spring classes explored themes such as: Legionnaires Disease, Lead poisoning, and environmental tobacco smoke.